Optimization Techniques for Real-Time Visual Object Detection and Tracking

Dissertation

der Fakultät für Informations- und Kognitionswissenschaften
der Eberhard-Karls-Universität Tübingen
zur Erlangung des Grades eines
Doktors der Naturwissenschaften
(Dr. rer. nat.)

vorgelegt von
Dipl.-Ing. André Treptow
aus Siegen

Tübingen
2007

Bibliografische Information der Deutschen Nationalbibliothek

Die Deutsche Nationalbibliothek verzeichnet diese Publikation in der
Deutschen Nationalbibliografie; detaillierte bibliografische Daten sind
im Internet über http://dnb.d-nb.de abrufbar.

ISBN 978-3-8325-1556-0

Logos Verlag Berlin
Comeniushof, Gubener Str. 47,
10243 Berlin
Tel.: +49 030 42 85 10 90
Fax: +49 030 42 85 10 92
INTERNET: http://www.logos-verlag.de

Tag der mündlichen Qualifikation: 14.02.2007
Dekan: Prof. Dr. Michael Diehl
1. Berichterstatter: Prof. Dr. Andreas Zell
2. Berichterstatter: Prof. Dr.-Ing. Dr.-Ing. E.h. Wolfgang Straßer

Abstract

This thesis addresses the problem of visual object detection and tracking in real-time. The implementation of vision as a sensor modality for machines has an increasing number of applications but introduces a number of problems that have to be solved in order to provide robust and fast vision systems. The performance of the systems depends on imaging conditions (light conditions, sensor noise, viewing angle, etc.) so that usually very complex solutions are needed. On the other hand the routines often have to be implemented on processors with reduced computational resources which can be found e.g. in mobile robots and in embedded systems. Therefore, one has to find a trade-off between runtime and accuracy of the vision system which results in an optimization problem.

In this thesis new combinations of vision and optimization are studied and new ideas from the field of heuristic optimization are used in order to solve the task of object detection and tracking. First, two different combinations of evolutionary search and machine learning are proposed in order to improve the robustness and the time complexity of visual object detection. It is shown that the new methods are able to learn classifiers for object detection that use a low number of image features while keeping a high detection rate. The second part of the thesis deals with the problem of tracking objects in image sequences. A probabilistic tracking algorithm is extended using ideas from the field of heuristic optimization. Here, it is shown that the runtime of the algorithm can be reduced without decreasing the tracking performance drastically. Finally, a complete system to detect and track people in thermal images on a mobile robot is introduced and evaluated. Different measurement models that use contour and gray features are proposed and compared. It is shown that the methods are suitable to detect people in thermal images on a mobile robot in real-time.

ii

Kurzfassung

Diese Arbeit befasst sich mit der Problematik der echtzeitfähigen Erkennung und Verfolgung von Objekten in Bildsequenzen. Die Implementierung dieser visuellen Routinen als Sensormodalität auf Maschinen wird immer häufiger in verschiedenen Bereichen angewendet, führt aber auch zu einer Vielzahl von Problemen, die betrachtet werden müssen, um robuste und laufzeitoptimierte Systeme zu entwickeln. Die Leistung der Systeme ist auf der einen Seite stark abhängig von den Bedingung im Bild (wie z.b. Lichtverhältnisse, Sensorrauschen, Blickwinkel, usw.), und verlangt daher nach sehr aufwendigen Lösungen. Auf der anderen Seite sollen diese aber auf Prozessoren mit stark reduzierter Rechenleistung, wie z.b. auf mobilen Robotern und Steuergeräten, eingesetzt werden. Deshalb muss oftmals ein Kompromiss zwischen Laufzeit und Genauigkeit der Algorithmen gefunden werden. Dieses Problem kann somit auch als Optimierungsproblem formuliert werden.

In dieser Arbeit werden Algorithmen zur Lösung von heuristischen Optimierungsproblemen auf dem Gebiet der visuellen Objekterkennung und -verfolgung eingesetzt und untersucht. Um die Leistung und Zeitkomplexität der Objekterkennung zu verbessern, werden zunächst zwei verschiedene Kombinationen von Evolutionärer Suche und maschinellen Lernalgorithmen vorgestellt und ausgewertet. Es wird gezeigt, dass mit den entwickelten Verfahren neue Klassifikatoren zur Objekterkennung erstellt werden können, welche eine geringere Anzahl von Merkmalen im Bild verwenden und gleichzeitig eine hohe Detektionsleistung garantieren. Der zweite Teil der Arbeit beschäftigt sich dann mit der Verfolgung von Objekten in Bildern über die Zeit. Hier wird ein probabilistischer Algorithmus mit Ansätzen aus dem Bereich der heuristischen Optimierung erweitert. Es wird gezeigt, dass die Laufzeit des Algorithmus mit den vorgestellten Erweiterungen ohne drastische Einbußen in der Detektionsleistung und Objektstabilität verringert werden kann. Im letzten Teil der Arbeit wird schließlich ein komplettes System zur Erkennung und Verfolgung von Personen in Infrarotbildern auf einem mobilen Roboter vorgestellt. Hier werden drei verschiedene Messmodelle, welche Kontur und Grauwertmerkmale in Bildern verwenden, entwickelt und verglichen. Es wird dargestellt, dass die vorgestellten Methoden zur robusten Erkennung von Personen im Infrarotbild geeignet und in Echtzeit auf einem mobilen Roboter einsetzbar sind.

Danksagung

Diese Arbeit entstand während meiner Tätigkeit als Wissenschaftlicher Mitarbeiter am Lehrstuhl für Rechnerarchitektur der Universität Tübingen. Mein besonderer Dank gilt zunächst meinem Doktorvater Prof. Dr. Andreas Zell für die Betreuung der Arbeit und die Bereitstellung der erforderlichen Mittel. Ebenso danke ich Prof. Dr.-Ing. Dr.-Ing. E.h. Wolfgang Straßer für die Übernahme des Zweitgutachtens. Claudia Walter, Klaus Beyreuther und Kurt Langenbach danke ich für die reibungslose Verwaltung und Administration.

Ich möchte allen Kollegen am Lehrstuhl Rechnerarchitektur für das gute Arbeitsklima und die erfolgreiche Zusammenarbeit danken, insbesondere Holger Fröhlich, Patrick Heinemann, Achim Lilienthal, Nora Speer, Christian Spieth, Felix Streichert, Hashem Tamimi, Holger Ulmer und Jörg Wegner. Ein besonderer Dank geht an Holger Fröhlich, Patrick Heinemann und Christian Spieth für die Korrektur der ersten Version meiner Arbeit und an Jörg Wegner für die gemeinsame Zeit in A 312.

Einen großen Beitrag zum Gelingen dieser Arbeit leisteten die Untersuchungen, die ich während meines Forschungsaufenthaltes am Institut Applied Autonomous Sensor Systems an der Universität Örebro in Schweden im Zuge eines Marie Curie Stipendiums der EU durchführen konnte. Hier möchte ich besonders Henrik Andreasson, Grzegorz Cielniak, Tom Duckett und Malin Lindquist für die gute Zusammenarbeit, die interessanten wissenschaftlichen Diskussionen und ihre große Hilfsbereitschaft danken.

Ein großer Dank gilt schließlich meiner Frau, Sandra Thiele-Treptow, die mein Mittelpunkt und Halt ist, und meinen Eltern, Brigitte und Klaus-Peter Treptow, die mir alles möglich gemacht haben und die immer für mich da sind.

Contents

Chapter 1

Introduction

1.1 Motivation

Among different sensor modalities, an image sensor (vision) provides one of the richest sources of information about the environment. The processing of visual information seems very natural to us since we mainly rely on visual information to perceive our surroundings. Our visual system is highly specialized and the process of sensing seems to be a concurrent task that can be solved without any apparent effort. The implementation of vision as a sensor modality for machines, which is known as Computer Vision, is an active and ongoing area of research and has many real-world applications, like:

- Intelligent transportation and driver assistance systems: detecting obstacles [83], vehicles [135], traffic signs [10], pedestrians [126], license plates [28] etc.

- Mobile Robotics: detecting and recognizing people [160] and objects [7], visual navigation [36].

- Human-Computer Interfaces: gesture recognition [162], face detection [167], and face recognition [172].

- Photography and smart cameras: object detection can be used on digital cameras for automatic focusing, color balancing and zooming on target objects [23].

- Automatic surveillance: tracking multiple people and monitoring activities with a stationary camera [60], [57].

- Smart rooms and human motion capturing: extracting a full human body model from image sequences with a static camera [96].

Detecting and tracking of certain objects in real world scenarios is a challenging task due to a variety of problems that are introduced by different imaging conditions (light,

1

noise), different viewing angles, and different image appearance of objects from the same class. This task becomes even more difficult if one wants to implement visual routines in systems that have restricted computational resources, like autonomous mobile robots or embedded systems in a car. The reduced computational power is a result of the strict requirements that are made for hardware in these systems: small and cheap devices, low power consumption, operation under temperatures that range from -40°C to 90°C, etc. On the other hand, real-time performance is necessary especially in security systems and the process of object detection and classification has to be very robust since a single false classification could be fatal.

A canonical definition of a real-time system is given by Gillies [5]: "A real-time system is one in which the correctness of the computations not only depends upon the logical correctness of the computation but also upon the time at which the result is produced. If the timing constraints of the system are not met, system failure is said to have occurred." The time that is needed by a software or hardware system to produce a number of outputs from a set of associated inputs is often called response time. Thus, in an image processing task or system where inputs are updated with the frame rate of a certain image sensor (e.g. 25Hz) a real-time process must produce results within this bounded response time of e.g. 40ms. Algorithms that are used for image processing have to guarantee this upper bound in order to meet the real-time constraint. Therefore, in order to develop a fast and robust vision system, one always has to find a trade-off between runtime and accuracy of the system which results in an optimization problem.

In the field of heuristic optimization many sophisticated approaches were developed that are able to find (sub-)optimal solutions in constrained, multi-dimensional and multi-modal environments. In this thesis, new combinations of vision and optimization are studied on the problem of visual object detection and tracking. The main goal of this thesis is to develop robust methods for real-time environments by applying new ideas from the field of heuristic optimization. Two areas of application are analyzed in more detail. One area is the selection of good and distinctive image features that can be used to build robust classifiers. Here, optimization is used offline to find an optimal set of features. Another area for the application of heuristic optimization is the tracking process itself. The common probabilistic Condensation tracking algorithm shares a lot of similarities with the dynamic optimization problem so that in this thesis it will be studied how the tracking process can be improved by using techniques that were developed in the field of heuristic optimization.

1.2 Thesis contributions

The contributions of this thesis concern the problem of detecting and tracking of objects in images in real-time. New methods that combine heuristic optimization and machine vision are developed and evaluated in unconstrained real-world image scenarios. The three main contributions of the thesis are as follows:

Combination of machine learning and evolutionary search to improve real time object detection. Two different combinations of evolutionary search and machine learning techniques are proposed and evaluated in order to improve the robustness and time complexity of visual object detection. Evolutionary search is used to select promising and computationally cheap image features from a large set of possible features. These features are used to automatically learn classifiers for object detection.

Extension of a probabilistic tracking algorithm with operations from the field of heuristic optimization. The similarities between a probabilistic tracking algorithm (Condensation, Particle Filter) and Evolutionary Algorithms are identified and two different ideas from the field of heuristic optimization are integrated in the tracking algorithm. It is shown that better tracking performance can be achieved while at the same time using less number of computational expensive measurements in the image.

New techniques to detect people in thermal images on a mobile robot. Three different models to detect and track people in thermal images on a mobile robot are developed. The advantages of processing thermal images are highlighted and the different models are compared. It is shown that the proposed method can be applied in situations where standard techniques based e.g. on color image processing often fail (person is far away or does not face the robot).

1.3 Thesis outline

The thesis is structured as follows:

Chapter 2 introduces basic algorithms from the field of optimization and machine learning that are used in the following chapters. Heuristic optimization techniques like Evolutionary Algorithms and algorithms for learning classifiers like Adaboost and Support Vector Machines are introduced in more detail.

The problem of detecting objects in images is addressed in Chapter 3. After a general introduction to the problem, different solutions that were proposed in the literature are described. The chapter focuses on the usage of methods for learning classifiers based on certain image features.

In Chapter 4 two new approaches for object detecting using learning classifiers are described and analyzed. Here, Evolutionary Algorithms are combined with Adaboost and Support Vector Classification.

After a target object was detected in an image, object tracking strategies are applied in order to predict and update the target position over a consecutive image sequence. Object tracking is introduced in Chapter 5 where the two common approaches, the Kalman filter and the probabilistic Condensation algorithm are illustrated.

Chapter 6 describes and compares several new extensions that have been developed in this thesis to improve and speed up object tracking methods based on the Condensation algorithm. The basic analogy between Condensation and Evolutionary Algorithms in dynamic environments is described and methods from the field of heuristic optimization are applied to Condensation tracking. A detailed evaluation of the proposed approaches is presented in the last part of the chapter.

Chapter 7 shows a complete system that was implemented in order to detect, track and identify people on a mobile robot using a thermal and a color camera. In this chapter a new measurement model based on contours is developed and compared to a feature based classifier that was introduced in the first part of the thesis.

The thesis concludes with Chapter 8, which gives a brief summary and an outlook on topics that are left for future research.

Chapter 2

Optimization and Machine Learning Techniques

2.1 Introduction

In this chapter, basic methods and algorithms from the field of optimization and machine learning are introduced. The chapter is mainly split into two parts. The first part introduces the field of optimization and describes two nature inspired heuristic optimization techniques (Evolutionary Algorithms and Particle Swarms) in more detail. The second part is concerned with methods for automatic supervised learning from examples. Here, Support Vector Classification and Adaboost learning are introduced. After a short comparison of Boosting and Support Vector Classification two methods are described that deal with dimensionality and runtime reduction in learning and classification. The reduced set method has been proposed in order to speed up Support Vector classification and the problem of selecting an optimal subset of features to reduce the dimensionality of the search space is introduced. All basic algorithms that are described in this chapter are utilized in the latter part of this thesis to address the problem of visual object detection and tracking.

2.2 Optimization and nature inspired heuristics

The field of optimization deals with the determination of optimal solutions under certain constraints. The general problem of optimization can be defined as follows [51]: Given a number of $m + 1$ real valued functions

$$f : \mathbb{R}^n \to \mathbb{R}, \ g_i : \mathbb{R}^n \to \mathbb{R}, \ (i = 1, ..., m) \tag{2.1}$$

we search for the points $\mathbf{x} = (x_1, x_2, ..., x_n) \in \mathbb{R}^n$, which satisfy

$$g_i(x) \leq 0, \ (i = 1, ..., m) \tag{2.2}$$

5

and minimize $z = f(\mathbf{x})$. The function $f(\mathbf{x})$ is called objective function, and the inequalities $g_i(\mathbf{x}) \leq 0$ are called constraints. The set

$$\mathcal{M} := \{\mathbf{x} \in \mathbb{R}^n | g_i(\mathbf{x}) \leq 0, \ (i = 1, ..., m)\} \tag{2.3}$$

which is defined by the constraints is named search space. Points in the search space where the objective function is minimal are called optima. Depending on the objective function, constraints and nature of the search space one differentiates between linear, non-linear, discrete and combinatorial optimization problems. Heuristics for solving optimization problems are methods to "construct" (near) optimal solutions rather than explicitly calculate the exact solution. Heuristics are usually applied if no close solution to a problem exists or if the solution cannot be determined in reasonable time.

A powerful heuristic for solving optimization problems are Evolutionary Algorithms which will be illustrated in the next section.

2.2.1   Evolutionary Algorithms

An Evolutionary Algorithm [25] operates on a set P of possible solutions of the optimization problem. This set is called population and each solution or individual in the population represents exactly one point in the search space of the problem. To evaluate the quality of each individual, a fitness function is defined which represents the objective function of the optimization problem. In the first step, a start population, which contains usually randomly initialized individuals, is generated and evaluated by the fitness function. After that, individuals are selected from the actual population to build up a population P'. Different selection strategies exist and are described in the following section. Solutions in the population P' are modified by the application of two different operators: recombination and mutation. Recombination exchanges parts between individuals while the mutation operator changes certain parts of a solution. All individuals in P' are then evaluated and replace together with the old population P_t a new set P_{t+1}. This process of selection, recombination, mutation and replacement is iterated over a number of timesteps (each step is called generation) so that the solutions are gradually adapted to the given problem. The EA terminates if a certain termination criterion (e.g. fixed number of iterations or given quality of solution is reached) is met. Another typical termination criterion is the convergence of the algorithm: The EA is converged, if no new individuals can be produced by the application of recombination and mutation. This is the case if all individuals are equal or are too similar to generate solutions that are not already part of the actual population. A premature convergence before reaching the optimum or a sufficiently good approximation is not wanted in this context. The pseudo-code notation of an Evolutionary Algorithm is given in figure 2.1.

Following [45], Evolutionary Algorithms offer certain advantages over classical methods for solving optimization problems:

```
procedure EA(P) : returns P
begin
  t:=0;
  initialize(P(0));
  evaluate(P(0));
  repeat
    P' := select(P(t));
    recombine(P');
    mutate(P');
    evaluate(P');
    P(t + 1) := replace(P(t), P');
    t:=t+1;
  until termination;
end
```

Figure 2.1: Evolutionary Algorithm

- Conceptual Simplicity: Evolutionary Algorithms are all based on the same basic concept of iterative adaptation via recombination, mutation and selection. The difficulty lies in the determination of the fitness function and the specification of the evolutionary operators.

- Large number of applications: In principle, all problems that can be formulated as a function optimization problem can be addressed with EAs. The nature of the search space (discrete, continuous, etc.) is irrelevant. Therefore, EAs are especially suitable for problems that cannot be solved by numerical methods e.g. due to an indifferentiable objective function.

- Possibility to integrate problem specific knowledge and combination with other methods: The performance of an EA can be increased by introducing special problem specific information. This can be done e.g. by defining operators for recombination and mutation that are adapted to the given problem. Instead of using random initialization the individuals can be initialized using problem specific knowledge and information about the possible location of optimal solutions in the search space.

- Parallelism: EAs sample the search space massively parallel and are thus very suitable for different kinds of parallelization strategies.

- Robustness against dynamic changes: In many practical applications conditions can change during the optimization process. An EA is able to adapt dynamically to a changing environment so that feasible solutions can be adapted over time. The field of application of EAs to dynamic environments became very popular in the last years where different extensions for EAs in dynamic optimization had been proposed.

- Ability to self-adaption: Parameters of an EA can be added to each individual so that they are optimized by the evolutionary process, too. In contrast to this ability, classical methods usually operate on a fixed and pre-defined set of parameters.

In the past, different approaches within the class of Evolutionary Algorithm have been developed, which mainly differ in the choice of the coding of individuals: Genetic Algorithms [64] use a binary coding, Evolution Strategies [108] operate on real-value coded continuous vectors, Evolutionary Programming [46] are used to optimize finite state machines and Genetic Programming [76] uses computer programs that are represented as trees. Depending on the type of Evolutionary Algorithm there exist different operators (especially different types of recombination and mutation). An overview over typical operations used in Evolutionary Algorithms is given in the following.

Selection operators for EAs

In the literature different strategies to select individuals that are used to build the next generation can be found:

- Random selection: Each individual is chosen randomly with the same probability.

- Fitness proportionate selection: The probability $p(i)$ to select an individual i is proportional to its fitness $f(i)$:

$$p(i) = \frac{f(i)}{\sum\limits_{j \in P} f(j)} \tag{2.4}$$

- Rank-based selection: the selection probability is proportional to the rank of the fitness value. The exact numerical value is not necessary. Linear rank selection assigns a selection probability $p(i)$ that is calculated by a linear function to each individual i: Individuals are sorted by their fitness value in descending order first and are then selected with probability

$$p(i) = \left(\eta^+ - (\eta^+ - \eta^-) \cdot \frac{i-1}{\lambda - 1}\right)/\lambda, 1 \leq \eta^+ \leq 2, \; \eta^- = 2 - \eta^+. \tag{2.5}$$

The factor λ denotes the size of the population, and the constants η^+ and η^- define the range of values of the linear function. The individual with the highest fitness value gets a selection probability of $p(1) = \eta^+/\lambda$ while the worst individual is selected with $p(\lambda) = \eta^-/\lambda$.

- Tournament selection: In a first step, a group of k individuals is chosen randomly. After that, the individual with the highest fitness value in the group is selected.

Replacement operators for EAs

The replacement method defines which individuals from the population are replaced by their offsprings in the next generation. Replacement requires a selection process because one has to select individuals from the current and the offspring population that should form the next population. Several strategies for replacement exist:

- Generational replacement: The current population is replaced completely by their offsprings.

- Steady-State replacement: Instead of replacing the whole population at the end of each generation of the EA, parents are replaced by their offsprings directly after they are created. Different methods for parent replacement exist e.g. replace parent if offspring has better fitness or replace oldest individual in the population. Offsprings that are directly inserted into the population can be selected for recombination and mutation in the next step so that in a steady state EA no fixed generations exist any longer.

- (μ, λ)-replacement: The best μ individuals out of $\lambda > \mu$ offpsrings are selected to replace μ parents.

- $(\mu + \lambda)$-replacement: The best μ individuals out of the sum of μ parents and λ offsprings are selected for the next generation.

Recombination operators for EAs

This section shortly describes some of the most popular recombination operators. One-point-, n-point- and uniform-crossover usually operate on two individuals $\mathbf{a}$ and $\mathbf{b}$ that are binary coded ($\mathbf{a}, \mathbf{b} \in \{0, 1\}^l$) and create two child individuals $\mathbf{a}', \mathbf{b}'$. Discrete and intermediate crossover have been proposed for real value coded individuals in Evolution Strategies. The probability for the application of a crossover operator is specified by the crossover-rate p_c. In Genetic Algorithms p_c is usually relatively high ($p_c > 0.5$) while crossover is used in Evolution Strategies as a background operator with low probability.

One-point-crossover: This operator divides $\mathbf{a}$ and $\mathbf{b}$ at a randomly chosen point p into two segments. From these segments, $\mathbf{a}', \mathbf{b}'$ are created by

$$a_i' = \left\{ \begin{array}{lll} a_i & : & i \leq p \\ b_i & : & i > p \end{array} \right. , \qquad b_i' = \left\{ \begin{array}{lll} b_i & : & i \leq p \\ a_i & : & i > p \end{array} \right.$$

N-point-crossover: One-point-crossover can be generalized to n-point-crossover in the following way: after choosing n different crossover points randomly, the bit-strings of two parents are crossed between these points in order to build two child individuals.

Uniform-crossover: Here, a binary vector $m \in \{0,1\}^l$ is initialized randomly. The value of entry m_i of the crossover-mask m defines from which parent the ith entry is copied to the child individual:

$$a_i' = \begin{cases} b_i & : & m_i = 1 \\ a_i & : & otherwise \end{cases}, \qquad b_i' = \begin{cases} a_i & : & m_i = 1 \\ b_i & : & otherwise \end{cases} \qquad (2.6)$$

Discrete and intermediate crossover: These operators perform a recombination between two randomly selected and real value coded individuals $a, b \in R^n$. The discrete crossover generates a child individual a' by choosing either a_i or b_i randomly for the vector component a_i'. Intermediate crossover calculates the arithmetic mean between a_i and b_i or uses a random weight $\rho \in [0, 1]$ to place the child in between a and b (generalized intermediate):

$$a_i' = \begin{cases} a_i \vee b_i & : & \text{discrete} \\ a_i + 0.5 \cdot (b_i - a_i) & : & \text{intermediate} \\ a_i + \rho \cdot (b_i - a_i) & : & \text{generalized intermediate} \end{cases} \qquad (2.7)$$

Instead of using the fixed value b_i for recombination of all vector components, a so called panmictic crossover has been proposed where a new individual z is chosen randomly for each component to act as a crossover partner.

Mutation operators for EAs

In a binary bit-vector coding, individuals are commonly mutated using a random bit flip or an inversion operation. Bit flip mutation simply changes a small number of randomly chosen bits in the individual. The inversion operator chooses two random points and the substring between these points in the bit vector are reversed. Mutation plays only a secondary role in Genetic Algorithms and is often used to diversify the population in order to prevent premature convergence into local optima.

In contrast to Genetic Algorithms, mutation is used as a primary operation in Evolution Strategies. Mutation on a real valued vector $x \in$ can be realized by adding a random constant that is normally distributed:

$$x_i' = x_i + N(0, \sigma_i), i = 1...l, \qquad (2.8)$$

with $N(0, \sigma_i)$ denoting a normally distributed random number with zero mean and standard deviation σ_i which is called mutation step length. The mutation step length can be included in the individual to enable self-adaptation of this parameter:

$$\sigma_i' = \sigma_i \exp(\tau' N(0,0) + \tau N_i(0,1)), \qquad (2.9)$$
$$x_i' = x_i + N(0, \sigma_i'), \ i = 1...l. \qquad (2.10)$$

Here, τ and τ' define global and individual step sizes for the mutation of the step length σ_i. Other mutation strategies that are used to alter a real-value coded vector are e.g. covariance-matrix adaptation CMA [58],[59] or main vector adaptation MVA [106].

2.2.2 Particle Swarm Optimization

Eberhart and Kennedy developed a heuristic that searches for optima by simulating the nature of collective behavior in flocking birds ([71], [72]). Birds in the swarm fly around while trying to find an optimal position (landing position, food, etc.). The individuals do not change their flight randomly but define their direction and velocity based on their own flight experience and that of their neighbors. Each individual holds its own optimal position within the swarm.

The Particle Swarm algorithm (PSO) adapts the swarm behavior of flying birds to the solution of an optimization problem: Each individual (particle) is a vector with dimension D and represents a possible solution that "flies" in the search space. The i-th particle $\mathbf{x}_i = (x_{i,1}, x_{i,2}, x_{i,3}, ..., x_{i,D})^T$ has its own "flight velocity" $\mathbf{v}_i = (v_{i,1}, v_{i,2}, v_{i,3}, ..., v_{i,D})^T$ and stores its best known position $\mathbf{p}_i = (p_{i,1}, p_{i,2}, p_{i,3}, ..., p_{i,D})^T$. The quality of a solution at the particles actual position is measured in analogy to EAs by a problem specific fitness function. In each step within the PSO algorithm, a new position for each particle is calculated:

$$x_{i,d} = x_{i,d} + v_{i,d}, \ d = 1...D. \tag{2.11}$$

The velocity $\mathbf{v}_i$ is adjusted before:

$$v_{i,d} = v_{i,d} + c_1 \cdot U(0,1) \cdot (p_{i,d} - x_{i,d}) + c_2 \cdot U(0,1) \cdot (p_d^* - x_{i,d}) \tag{2.12}$$

where c_1 and c_2 are positive constants and $U(0,1)$ generates uniformly distributed random values in $[0,1]$. The position $\mathbf{p}^*$ is the global best position that was reached by the population. A selection mechanism is not used in particle swarms and individuals are usually initialized randomly. The standard PSO algorithm does not use any selection or replacement operators on the whole population. The pseudo-code notation of PSO is depicted in figure 2.2.

A comparison between Evolutionary Algorithms and Particle Swarm optimization can be found in [8] and some extensions to the original algorithm are described e.g. in [127], [9].

```
procedure PSO(Number of particles N) :
returns gobal best particle: p*, best fitness: global_best_f
begin
   global_best_f := 0;
   for i:= 1 to N
      initialize_random(x_i, v_i);
      p_i := x_i;
      local_best_f_i := fitness(x_i);
      if local_best_f_i > global_best_f then
         global_best_f := local_best_f_i;
         p* := x_i;
      endif
   endfor
   repeat
      for i:= 1 to N
         v_i:= update_velocity(x_i, v_i, p_i, p*);
         x_i:= x_i + v_i;
         if fitness(x_i) > local_best_f_i then
            local_best_f_i := fitness(x_i);
            p_i := x_i;
         endif
         if fitness(x_i) > global_best_f then
            global_best_f := fitness(x_i);
            p* := x_i;
         endif
      endfor
   until termination;
end
```

Figure 2.2: Particle Swarm Optimization.

2.3 Learning Classifiers

In supervised learning, we are given m training examples

$$(\mathbf{x}_1, y_1), ..., (\mathbf{x}_m, y_m) \in \mathcal{X} \times \mathcal{Y}. \tag{2.13}$$

for some unknown function $f : \mathcal{X} \to \mathcal{Y}$, where $\mathbf{x}_i \in \mathcal{X}$ are called patterns whose components are usually discrete or real-valued features and the y_i values are drawn from a discrete set of classes $\mathcal{Y} = \{1, ..., K\}$. In the following we are interested in binary classification, so that $\mathcal{Y} = \{-1, 1\}$. The learning algorithm outputs a classifier $h(\mathbf{x})$ which is a hypothesis about the true function f. The classifier should be able to generalize to unseen patterns in a way that for a new pattern $\mathbf{x}_{new} \in \mathcal{X}$ a prediction $y_{new} \in \mathcal{Y}$ can be generated such that $y_{new} = f(x_{new})$. In the following, two methods (Boosting and Support Vector Classification, which will be used in this thesis, are described in more detail. In chapter 3 it is then shown how these methods are applied to the problem of detecting objects in images.

2.3.1 Boosting

The main idea of Boosting [116] is to combine a number of T simple classifiers to form the final hypothesis:

$$h(\mathbf{x}) = \sum_{t=1}^{T} \alpha_t h_t(\mathbf{x}). \tag{2.14}$$

Each h_t is called a "weak" classifier which means that the classification performance of h_t has to be just a little bit better than a random guess. The combination of a number of weak classifiers improves ("boosts") the classification performance compared to each single h_t. The α_t denotes a weight for each classifier and both α_t and h_t have to be learned with the Boosting algorithm. The idea of Boosting arose from PAC (probably approximately correct) learning [149] and Schapire [115] has been the first who developed a boosting algorithm with polynomial runtime. This algorithm had been improved and Freund and Schapire [49] introduced the Adaboost (adaptive boosting) algorithm which is depicted in figure 2.3. The algorithm is initialized with a number of training examples (see equation 2.13) and a non negative weight w_i for each example. The weights are uniformly distributed at the beginning. The algorithm iterates over a number of T rounds and in each iteration one weak classifier is trained based on the weighted training set. The factor α_t is calculated using the training error of the weak classifier so that a classifier with higher training error receives a lower impact in the linear combination of all hypotheses. Each weight w_i is then updated in way that correctly classified examples get a lower weight than missclassified patterns. The idea of iterative reweighting the training set is central to Adaboost and guarantees that in each round a weak classifier is chosen that has a lower classification error on examples which had been missclassified before. Thus, the algorithm focuses on the "harder" and therefore more informative patterns.

---

procedure Adaboost(Rounds T, Training set $S = \{(\mathbf{x}_i, y_i)\}$, $i = 1..N)$:

returns Strong classifier $h(x) := \sum_{t=1}^{T} \dfrac{\alpha_t}{\sum_{r=1}^{T} \alpha_r} h_t(\mathbf{x})$

begin
    for i:=1 **to** N **do**
        $w_{1,i} := \dfrac{1}{N}$;
    endfor
    for t:=1 **to** T **do**
        Normalize all weights $w_{t,i}$;
        Train classifier h_j with error $\epsilon_j = \sum_i w_{t,i} |h_j(x_i) - y_i|$;
        $\alpha_t := \dfrac{1}{2} \log \dfrac{1 - \epsilon_t}{\epsilon_t}$;
        Update weights: $w_{t+1,i} := w_{t,i} e^{-\alpha_t y_n h_t(\mathbf{x}_n)}$;
    endfor
end

Figure 2.3: Adaboost learning algorithm as proposed in [49].

In principle, every known classifier can be used for h_t. Most applications used decision trees or decision stumps (see e.g. [41, 40]). Decision trees are hierarchical classifiers that split the input space recursively into partitions and a decision stump is a single level decision tree that splits the input space only once. Other classifiers that are used together with boosting are e.g. Neural Networks [125] or Nearest Neighbor Classifiers [48]. Characteristic for learning classifier ensembles with Adaboost is the exponentially reduced training error of the ensemble as the number of weak classifiers is increased. At the same time, the weighted training error of each single weak classifier increases because the algorithm concentrates on more difficult training patterns. As long as the training error of each weak classifier is less than 0.5 and therefore better than a guess, it is guaranteed that the error of the final strong classifier is reduced further. Figure 2.4 illustrates the typical development of the error rates. Schapire et al. [117] analyzed the generalization error of a boosted classifier on unseen data in terms of the margins of training examples. The margin of an example $(\mathbf{x}, y)$ is defined for a boosted classifier h as:

$$\text{margin}_h(\mathbf{x}, y) = \frac{y h(\mathbf{x})}{\sum_t |\alpha_t|} = \frac{y \sum_t \alpha_t h_t(\mathbf{x})}{\sum_t |\alpha_t|}. \tag{2.15}$$

The margin is a value in $[-1, +1]$ which is positive if the example is classified correctly and which can be interpreted as a confidence measure for the classification result.

Schapire et al. proved that the upper bound of the generalization error is higher for larger margins on the training set and that the generalization error does not depend on the number of training rounds in Adaboost. The authors also showed that boosting increases the margins even after the training error has already reached zero so that the test error can be reduced further.

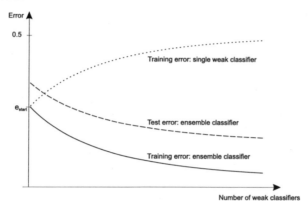

Figure 2.4: Typical, idealized characteristics of classification errors in Adaboost.

2.3.2 Support Vector Classification

The concept of Support Vector Machines (SVM) [150],[34],[151] has become very popular in the last years and has been applied to a broad range of learning problems. The main concept of Support Vector learning is to construct a classifier that maximizes the minimal distance between the closest points of the different classes and thus leads to high generalization on previously unseen data.

In case of linearly separable binary classes one can find a hyperplane which separates the two classes:

$$\langle \mathbf{w}, \mathbf{x_i} \rangle + b \geq +1 \qquad \text{if } y_i = +1 \qquad (2.16)$$
$$\langle \mathbf{w}, \mathbf{x_i} \rangle + b \leq -1 \qquad \text{if } y_i = -1 \qquad (2.17)$$

The points that lie exactly on the hyperplane satisfy $\langle \mathbf{w}, \mathbf{x_i} \rangle + b = 0$ where b is a constant threshold and $\mathbf{w}$ defines the normal to the plane. Usually there exists a family of separating hyperplanes and one wants to choose the one with that largest margin which means that it maximizes the minimal distance from the nearest training patterns to the plane (see

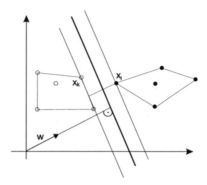

Figure 2.5: Maximal margin classifier for linear separable classes.

figure 2.5). In the following, it is assumed that we have two points x_l and x_k that lie on different sides of the hyperplane (see figure 2.5) and that satisfy the equalities

$$\langle \mathbf{w}, \mathbf{x_k} \rangle + b \;=\; +1 \tag{2.18}$$

$$\langle \mathbf{w}, \mathbf{x_l} \rangle + b \;=\; -1 \tag{2.19}$$

$$\Rightarrow \langle \mathbf{w}, (\mathbf{x_k} - \mathbf{x_l}) \rangle \;=\; 2. \tag{2.20}$$

The distances of x_l and x_k to the separating hyperplane are both minimal and it is possible that there are several points that have these properties. Maximizing the distance between these nearest points of different classes is the same as minimizing $\frac{1}{2}\langle \mathbf{w}, \mathbf{w} \rangle$ (see also e.g. [47]):

$$dist(\mathbf{x_k}, \text{hyperplane}) + dist(\mathbf{x_l}, \text{hyperplane}) \tag{2.21}$$

$$= \left(\frac{\langle \mathbf{w}, \mathbf{x_k} \rangle}{|\mathbf{w}|} + \frac{b}{|\mathbf{w}|} \right) - \left(\frac{\langle \mathbf{w}, \mathbf{x_l} \rangle}{|\mathbf{w}|} + \frac{b}{|\mathbf{w}|} \right) \tag{2.22}$$

$$= \frac{\langle \mathbf{w}, (\mathbf{x_k} - \mathbf{x_l}) \rangle}{|\mathbf{w}|} \tag{2.23}$$

$$= \frac{2}{|\mathbf{w}|} \tag{2.24}$$

This leads to the constrained optimization problem:

$$\text{minimize} \quad \frac{1}{2}\langle \mathbf{w}, \mathbf{w} \rangle \tag{2.25}$$

$$\text{subject to} \quad y_i(\langle \mathbf{w}, \mathbf{x}_i \rangle + b) \geq 1. \tag{2.26}$$

The problem can be solved by introducing positive Lagrange multipliers α_i to form a dual optimization problem:

$$\text{maximize} \quad \sum_{i=1}^{l} \alpha_i - \frac{1}{2} \sum_{i,j=1}^{l} \alpha_i \alpha_j y_i y_j \mathbf{x}_i \mathbf{x}_j \tag{2.27}$$

$$\text{subject to} \quad \alpha_i \geq 0 \tag{2.28}$$

$$\text{and} \quad \sum_{i=1}^{l} \alpha_i y_i = 0 \tag{2.29}$$

This problem can be solved via quadratic programming [52]. The parameters of the hyperplane $\mathbf{w}$ and b can be found via

$$\mathbf{w} = \sum_{i=1}^{l} \alpha_i y_i \mathbf{x}_i \tag{2.30}$$

$$y_m(\mathbf{w} \cdot \mathbf{x}_m + b)) = 1 \tag{2.31}$$

where $\mathbf{x}_m$ is any training pattern with $\alpha_m \neq 0$.

If the data cannot be separated linearly, a mapping Φ from the input space $\mathcal{X}$ to a higher dimensional feature space $\mathcal{F}$ is proposed (see also figure 2.6):

$$\Phi : \mathcal{X} \to \mathcal{F}, \; \mathbf{x} \to \Phi(\mathbf{x}). \tag{2.32}$$

The idea is to map the data into a new space in order to find a linear separating hyperplane there.

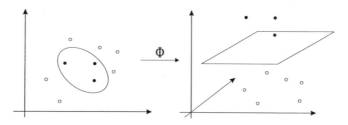

Figure 2.6: Mapping not linearly separable data from input space (left) to a linearly separable feature space (right).

By the usage of a kernel function

$$k(\mathbf{x}, \mathbf{x}') = \langle \Phi(\mathbf{x}), \Phi(\mathbf{x}') \rangle. \tag{2.33}$$

it is possible to compute dot products in feature spaces so that is it not necessary to work explicitly in the feature space (this is called the "kernel-trick").Nonlinear Support Vector classifier can then be defined as:

$$h(\mathbf{x}) = sgn\left(\sum_{i=1}^{l} \alpha_i y_i k(\mathbf{x}, \mathbf{x}_i) + b\right).$$ (2.34)

Training of the SVM is done by solving the following quadratic optimization problem:

$$\underset{\alpha}{\text{maximize}} \quad \sum_{i=1}^{l} \alpha_i - \frac{1}{2}\sum_{i,j=1}^{l} \alpha_i \alpha_j y_i y_j k(\mathbf{x}, \mathbf{x}_i)$$ (2.35)

$$\text{subject to} \quad 0 \le \alpha_i \le C, \ i = 1, ..., l, \ \sum_{i=1}^{l} \alpha_i y_i = 0$$ (2.36)

The positive parameter C is the upper bound of coefficients α_i and determines the trade-off between margin maximization and minimization of the training error. The value of C has to be adjusted to the problem: larger values for C correspond to higher penalties to errors. The training examples $\mathbf{x}_i$ with $\alpha_i > 0$ are called Support Vectors and lie on the margin. All other training examples are irrelevant and not used to build the final classifier.

Kernels that are often used in the literature are:

- Linear: $k(\mathbf{x}_i, \mathbf{x}_j) = \mathbf{x}_i^T \mathbf{x}_j$.

- Polynomial: $k(\mathbf{x}_i, \mathbf{x}_j) = (\gamma \mathbf{x}_i^T \mathbf{x}_j + r)^d$, $\gamma > 0$.

- Gaussian RBF: $k(\mathbf{x}_i, \mathbf{x}_j) = exp\left(\frac{-||\mathbf{x}_i - \mathbf{x}_j||^2}{2\sigma^2}\right)$.

2.3.3 Comparing Boosting and SVM

Boosting and SVM have been pointed out to be very similar concerning the attempt to either explicitly (SVM) or implicitly (Boosting) maximize the minimum margin of the classifier [50], [112]. According to [50], the differences between both approaches are due to the different norms that are used to calculate the margins, the different computational requirements and the different approaches to search in high-dimensional search spaces. Support Vector Machines use the l_2-norm (Euclidean distance) while Boosting applies the l_1-norm (Manhattan distance) which can result in large differences in the value of the margin in very high-dimensional spaces. As stated in [50], the margin produced by Adaboost can be much larger than for SVM's in case that the relevant number of weak hypotheses is sparse. The computational requirements differ because training a SVM uses quadratic programming while Boosting corresponds to linear programming which is less computational demanding. While SVM training uses kernels to efficiently search in high-dimensional search spaces, Boosting performs the computation explicitly in the feature space and relies on the fact that only a few hypotheses are necessary which can be found by a greedy search over the weak classifiers. The concept of kernels and weak classifiers is very different and thus results in different classifiers which operate in unequal spaces.

2.3.4 Reduced Set SVM

One disadvantage of SVM classification especially in real-time applications is the relative high number of support vectors that have to be evaluated for classification. In order to improve the evaluation speed, Burges [24] proposed a method to approximate the decision function using a lower number of so called reduced set vectors. According to [24] the reduced set vectors have the following properties:

- The vectors are computed for a trained SVM.

- The vectors do not equal training examples and do not necessary lie on the margin. Thus, they are not support vectors.

- Using reduced set vectors, the SVM decision rule is applied in the same way as using support vectors.

- The number of reduced set vectors is chosen a priori by hand.

- The method is applicable wherever the SVM method can be used.

Given the vector $\mathbf{w}$ which results from the SVM training

$$\mathbf{w} = \sum_{i=1}^{N_x} \gamma_i \Phi(\mathbf{x}_i) \qquad (2.37)$$

with $\gamma_i \in R$ and a number of N_x support vectors $\mathbf{x}_i \in R^n$, the reduced set method approximates $\mathbf{w}$ by

$$\mathbf{w}' = \sum_{i=1}^{N_z} \beta_i \Phi(\mathbf{z}_i) \qquad (2.38)$$

where N_z denotes the reduced number of vectors $\mathbf{z}_i \in R^n$ and $\beta_i \in R$. This approximation is done by minimizing the distance

$$\rho = ||\mathbf{w} - \mathbf{w}'|| \qquad (2.39)$$

Burges proposes the usage of a gradient descent method to minimize ρ based on a given number of reduced vectors N_z. Reduced set SVM classification is used to reduce the runtime in visual object detection. Further details are given in section 3.3.

2.3.5   Feature Selection

In many real-world applications and especially in computer vision problems, the data that has to be classified can be described by many different types of features which leads to a very high-dimensional input space. In order to reduce the dimensionality while achieving high classification accuracy one faces the problem to select a relevant feature subset. Support Vector machines do not provide an automatic way of relevance detection (unlike e.g. Gaussian Processes [53]) so that different algorithms for feature selection have been developed. The algorithms can be divided into filter and wrapper approaches (see [75], [19]). The filter approaches select features using a preprocessing step where certain relevance measures are used independently from the classification algorithm. Wrapper approaches, on the other hand, choose a feature subset by incorporating the results of the learning algorithm. A subset is used to train the classifier on the data set and the resulting generalization rate is used to evaluate the selected features. This procedure is usually executed iteratively with different subsets. The differences between wrapper and filter approaches are depicted in figure 2.7.

Wrapper approach

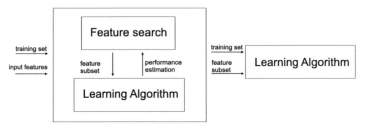

Filter approach

Figure 2.7: Wrapper and filter approaches in feature selection.

The Recursive feature elimination algorithm (RFE [55]) belongs to the wrapper approaches and will be outlined in the following. The algorithm maintains a set of features S which is initialized with the total number of features that are to be processed. A ranked feature list $\mathcal{F}$ is initialized as an empty set and used to save a number of selected features that are ranked by their relevance. RFE iterates over a number of steps and in each step a linear Support Vector machine is trained using $\mathcal{S}$ and the pattern training set. After that, a ranking criterion c_i is calculated for each feature i using the weight vector $\mathbf{w}$.

$$c_i = w_i^2, \ i = 1...n \tag{2.40}$$

$$\mathbf{w} = \sum_{k=1}^{l} \alpha_k y_k \mathbf{x}_k \tag{2.41}$$

The vector $\mathbf{w}$ together with the coefficients α_k are the result of the SVM learning process and have been introduced in section 2.3.2. The set $\{(\mathbf{x}_k, y_k)\}$ denotes the training set. Using w_i^2 as a ranking criterion is justified by the fact that a linear SVM minimizes $\frac{1}{2}\langle \mathbf{w}, \mathbf{w}\rangle$ (see section 2.3.2).

The feature with the best ranking criterion (minimal c_i) is inserted into $\mathcal{F}$ and deleted from $\mathcal{S}$. It is possible to remove more than one feature in each step to speed up the algorithm. The first m features in the final feature ranked list $\mathcal{F}$ define the best feature subset and are used to train the final classifier. Figure 2.3.5 shows the RFE algorithm in pseudo-code notation.

```
procedure RFE(𝒳, y) : returns ℛ
begin
    initialize feature subset 𝒮 = {1, 2, ..., n};
    subset of selected features ℛ = ∅;
    repeat
        𝒳' :=select(𝒳, 𝒮);
        α :=SMV_train(𝒳', y);
        w := ∑ₖ αₖyₖxₖ;
        cᵢ := wᵢ², i = 1...l;
        f :=argmin(c);
        ℛ := ℛ ∪ {𝒮(f)};
        𝒮 := 𝒮 − {f};
    until 𝒮 = ∅;
end
```

Figure 2.8: Recursive Feature Elimination as proposed in [55]

2.4 Summary

Basic concepts and commonly used algorithms from the field of optimization and machine learning have been addressed in this chapter. The first part focused on the description of Evolutionary Algorithms which are a powerful tool to search for optimal solutions in high-dimensional and multimodal search spaces. In the second part of this chapter Support Vector Machines and Adaboost were introduced for supervised learning of classifiers on a given data set. The techniques that have been described here are applied in the computer vision community to the problem of learning classifiers for object detection, which will be introduced in the next chapter. Feature selection plays an important role in the design of robust and fast image classifiers due to the high number of different visual features that can be observed. In this thesis, Evolutionary Algorithms are used in combination with Support Vector learning and Boosting to find optimal image feature subsets in order to improve the classification accuracy and decrease computational costs (see chapter 4). On the other hand, EAs and probabilistic methods for tracking objects in image sequences share a lot of similarities which are highlighted in chapter 6 in order to improve object tracking robustness in real-time scenarios.

Chapter 3

Learning Classifiers for Visual Object Detection

3.1 Introduction

Visual object detection is the task of determining parameters like position, scale and orientation of a certain object of interest in a single image observation. This is a natural process in human vision, which is very accurate while it is solved without any effort that detracts us from other tasks. However, the design of an artificial vision system that is able to detect objects is an unsolved challenge in computer research (Schneiderman and Kanade actually claimed in 2004 [122] that "in over 30 years of research in computer vision, progress has been limited" in automatic object detection).

In an artificial vision system the task of detecting objects in images is usually solved in two steps:

1. Train a two class classifier offline that is able to distinguish between the object of interest and background (non-objects). The training is often carried out using machine learning techniques that have been described in the previous chapter.

2. Evaluate the classifier online at each position and scale over the whole image to determine possible object locations.

This chapter deals with the first step, which is automatic learning of object classifiers on a given set of training images. First, the problem and the challenges of visual object detection are described together with a general introduction to the different approaches for solving the object detection problem. In the second part of the chapter, current state-of-the art methods, which have been widely-used, are described in more detail. Here, the main focus lies on methods that have been developed to reduce the computational complexity in order to work in real-world applications.

3.2   Visual Object Detection

Detecting objects in images is a challenging problem and an active area of research that
has to cope with a number of problems ([167, 123, 171]), due to:

- different viewing angles,

- different imaging conditions such as changing illumination and camera characteristics,

- occlusions that occur by other objects or background in a cluttered environment,

- variability in the appearance of objects in the same class (e.g. different appearances
  of faces), and

- different structural components that can be present or absent (e.g. eye-glass on a
  face)

A hard real-time constraint makes the problem even more challenging because one has to
find a good trade-off between high detection rates and runtime for image processing and
classification tasks. The task of object detection is related to the field of object recognition. Detecting an object is a two-class classification problem where we want to distinguish between a certain class of target objects (i.e. car, face, etc.) and the background.
Object recognition, on the other hand, tries to determine the identity of the detected object (e.g. identity of a person) to be able to distinguish between different objects from the
same class.

Following [171], the approaches for visual object detection can be classified into appearance based and feature based methods. In appearance based approaches, objects are
represented directly by their pixel intensities under different viewing conditions. Therefore, the vector that describes an object is usually very large, which can be disadvanta-
geous for the classification task. Methods such as principal component analysis (PCA)
have been used to reduce the dimensionality. Appearance based methods can be found in
[103, 136, 121, 123]. Different common approaches using Support Vector classification
are described in section 3.3.

Feature based methods, on the other hand, try to extract certain visual features to describe
the target object so that the resulting feature vector is usually more compact. The classification task can therefore be more efficient, at the expense of higher computational costs
to extract the features. Thus, the type of features that are used has to be chosen carefully
to achieve fast feature extraction and robust classification. Feature based methods usually
have less trouble in detecting objects that are slightly different from those in the training
set, so that smaller training sets can be used. Visual features that have been used in the
past are, for example, wavelet features [104], differential invariants [120], SIFT features

(scale invariant feature transform [109]), steerable Gaussian filters [118] or shape features [14, 15]. A current state-of-the art system that uses rectangular features to calculate differences between pixel values in gray images will be described in more detail in section 3.4.

Besides the choice of relevant features for object detection, the proposed methods differ in the approach that is used to learn templates and classify image patches. Most current systems either use SVM or Adaboost classification, which have been shown to be very robust without the need for using problem specific knowledge that depends on the types of objects to be classified. These methods are described in the following sections in more detail. However, especially for the problem of face detection one can find different approaches in the literature, including Neural Networks [56], Winnow learning [111, 6], maximum discrimination learning [33, 32], etc.

3.3 Object detection with Support Vector Machines

One of the first systems that was developed to detect faces in images using Support Vector learning was proposed in [103]. The system detected faces by scanning an image and classifying each sub-window using a SVM. The SVM was trained offline using a database of face and none-face images that had the size of 19x19 pixels. A second degree polynomial was used as a kernel function. The images were preprocessed in order to make the system robust to certain image variations: all pixels at the border of the window that did not contain parts of the face were removed and illumination correction followed by histogram equalization was used to compensate for different illumination conditions. After the SVM was trained, a step called bootstrapping was executed to improve the robustness of the classifier. The system was evaluated over a number of images that did not contain faces in order to use all false positive detections to re-train the SVM on the extended training set.

After the final SVM training step, the system detected faces in single images in the following way:

- Build an image-pyramid with different image scales.

- Cut 19x19 image patches out of every position in each scale.

- Preprocess the sub-window (masking, light correction).

- Classify the sub-window using SVM.

- Mark the sub-window in the image if classification is positive.

Most of the runtime of object detection systems that rely on SVMs is spent in the classification step which often uses more than 1000 support vectors. However, building the image pyramid and preprocessing each window are also expensive image processing tasks. Instead of using pixel gray values directly, Papageorgiou et al. [104] selected significant wavelet coefficients from a statistical analysis of the input training set. The compact representation was used to train a detector with SVMs for face and pedestrian detection.

In order to reduce the runtime of the classification task, Heisele et al. extended their work on face detection [61] and proposed a hierarchical classification with SVM [62]. They trained a number of hierarchical SVMs that use an increasing image resolution starting from 3x3 to 19x19 pixels. To reduce the dimension of the input space, a ranking method on PCA gray value features was proposed so that the total detection system was able to process an image of the size 320x240 in 259ms (Pentium IV, 1.8GHz) which is a speedup factor of 335 compared to single SVM classification. This seems to be a tremendous speedup but the detection was still 4 times slower than the detector by Viola and Jones (see section 3.4).

Runtime reduction is also the aim of the work of Romdhani et al. [110] who trained a reduced set SVM for face detection and compared the results to a standard SVM. Pixel gray values are used directly as image features. The authors introduced a sequential evaluation of the reduced set SVM which can be seen as a cascaded classification. Comparing their method to standard SVM classification, they reported substantial savings in computational time (speedup factor 30).

Rätsch et al. [114] extended this work by approximating the reduced set vectors with rectangular regions of the same gray value so that they can be calculated very quickly with an integral image (see section 3.4 for the definition of integral images). The approximation was done with a simulated annealing optimization process while in [113] the same authors proposed the usage of a wavelet transformation to perform this approximation.

The idea of approximating support vectors to speed up the classification process was also published by Kienzle et. al in [73]. Here the authors constrained the reduced support vectors so that they could be computed with separable convolutions. This method reduced the computational complexity from $O(h \cdot w)$ to $O(r \cdot (h + w))$ where w and h are the width and height of an image patch and r is a small number that was used to find a trade-off between runtime and classification accuracy.

3.4 Object detection with Adaboost

In 2001, Viola and Jones developed a framework for object detection that achieves high classification rates that are comparable to the best published results while running in real-time on standard PC hardware [155, 156, 157]. The work of Viola and Jones has three main contributions that result in an extremely fast object detection system. First, a new image representation which is called integral image has been proposed so that image features can be calculated very quickly. The second contribution is the application of Adaboost learning to construct an efficient classifier from a small number of features. Finally, the combination of several classifiers into a cascade is introduced in order to quickly reject large regions in the image that do not contain the target object. The work of Viola and Jones has become a standard tool for the construction of fast and reliable object detection systems in the computer vision community (see also section 3.4.4) and will therefore be described in more detail in the following sections.

3.4.1 Features in Integral Images

An integral image II over an image I contains at each image position (x, y) the sum of all pixel values of the image I in the rectangle between $(0, 0)$ and (x, y):

$$II(x, y) = \sum_{x' \leq x, y' \leq y} I(x', y') \tag{3.1}$$

The integral image can be calculated in one pass over the image I in the following way:

$$s(x, y) = s(x, y - 1) + I(x, y) \tag{3.2}$$
$$II(x, y) = II(x - 1, y) + s(x, y). \tag{3.3}$$

with $s(x, -1) = 0$ and $II(-1, y) = 0$.

With the use of an integral image, a sum of pixels within any rectangular image area can be calculated very quickly with only four array references: As one can see in figure 3.1, the sum of pixels in region D can be calculated by referencing the points a, b, c and d. The value at position a is the sum of pixels in region A, point b contains $A+B$, the value of c is $A+C$ and d contains the sum of pixels $A+B+C+D$. Thus, the sum in region D is $a + d - (c + b)$.

Due to the fast calculation of pixel sums, the integral image representation is very suitable for the real-time calculation of image features that consist of differences between rectangular image regions. Referring to the work of Papageorgiou et al. [104], Viola and Jones propose the use of four different types of such features, which are called "Haar-like" due to the fact that the feature response can be seen as a coefficient of a Haar-wavelet transformation. The four different features that represent edges, corners and lines are depicted

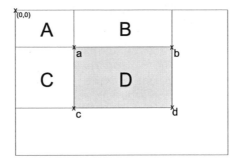

Figure 3.1: Calculating the pixel sum in region D with an integral image.

in figure 3.2. The sum of pixels in the white boxes are subtracted from the sum of pixels in the black areas. Despite the fast calculation, the rectangular features have also the advantage that they can be rescaled very easily. Thus, the classification of an image at different scales does not require the computationally more expensive calculation of an image pyramid any longer.

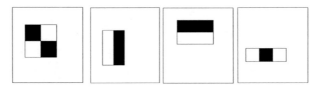

Figure 3.2: Four different types of rectangular features within their bounding box.

An image region of the size nxm contains much more possible features than pixels because the set of features is over-complete and many features can be redundant or irrelevant for exact classification. Therefore, one has to select a small number of distinctive features from the over-complete set. Viola and Jones propose the use of the Adaboost algorithm for feature selection and classifier construction at the same time. This method is described in the next section.

3.4.2 Adaboost for feature selection

The Adaboost algorithm (see section 2.3.1) can be used to learn an efficient classifier for object detection based on a collection of simple features in integral images. If each weak classifier uses only one single image feature then the boosting process selects a number of classifiers/features to classify a given set of positive and negative image examples. Viola and Jones use common linear threshold classifiers as weak learners:

$$h_j(x) = \left\{ \begin{array}{lll} 1 & : & \text{if } p_j f_j(x) < p_j \theta_j \\ 0 & : & \text{otherwise} \end{array} \right. \tag{3.4}$$

where θ_j is a threshold and p_j a parity indicating whether the feature f_j has to be greater or less than the threshold for a positive classification of the image sub-window x. Due to the fact that every weak classifier only has to be better than a guess, the calculation of the threshold is very simple: The mean value of the feature responses on the positive examples μ_{pos} and the mean value of the feature results on the negative examples μ_{neg} is determined first. The threshold is then calculated as

$$\theta_j = \frac{\mu_{pos} + \mu_{neg}}{2}. \tag{3.5}$$

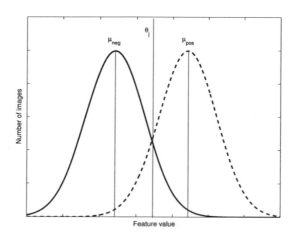

Figure 3.3: Idealized plot of the feature value distribution.

The selection of a weak classifier in each round of Adaboost is therefore done by an exhaustive search over all possible features at every position and scale in a given training image. For each feature, the classification threshold θ_j is determined and the classification error over the whole weighted image set is calculated. The classifier with the lowest error is chosen as the weak learner. Figure 2.3 shows the algorithm for boosting classifiers with single features. Note that the algorithm given here differs from the Adaboost algorithm in figure 2.3: the initialization of the weights depends on the number of positive and negative examples and each weak classifier consists of one single feature together with a linear threshold classifier. The weights are scaled such that the results of the final strong classifier are zero for negative classification and one for positive classification.

---

procedure FeatureAdaboost(Rounds T, Training set (x_i, y_i), $i = 1..N$, $y_i \in \{0, 1\}$) :

returns Strong classifier $h(x) = \begin{cases} 1 & : \quad \sum_{t=1}^{T} \alpha_t h_t(x) \geq 0.5 \sum_{t=1}^{T} \alpha_t \\ 0 & : \quad \text{otherwise} \end{cases}$

begin
   m := Number of negative examples;
   l := Number of positive examples;
   for i:=1 **to** N **do**
     if $y_i = 0$ **then**
       $w_{1,i} := \frac{1}{2m}$;
     else
       $w_{1,i} := \frac{1}{2l}$;
     endif
   endfor
   for t:=1 **to** T **do**
     Normalize all weights $w_{t,i}$
     For each feature j: Train classifier h_j with error $\epsilon_j = \sum_i w_{t,i} |h_j(x_i - y_i)|$;
     Choose h_t with lowest error ϵ_t;
     if x_i correctly classified **then**
       $e_i := 0$
     else
       $e_i := 1$
     endif
     $\beta_t := \frac{\epsilon_t}{1-\epsilon_t}$;
     $w_{t+1,i} := w_{t,i} \beta_t^{1-e_i}$
     $\alpha_t := log(\frac{1}{\beta_t})$
   endfor
end

Figure 3.4: Boosting classifiers with single features as proposed in [156].

3.4.3   Attentional cascades

The classification process can be speed up further by using a cascade of n different strong classifiers instead of a single one. In the first level of the cascade a classifier with a very low number of features which has a high detection rate and a high false positive rate is used to reject many sub-windows that do not contain the desired object. In case of a positive classification of the first level, a second classifier with a higher number of features is used to refine the classification and positive classified regions are passed to the next level and so on (see figure 3.5).

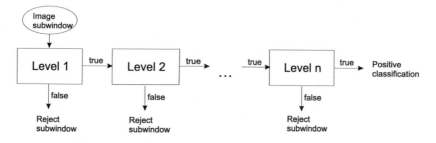

Figure 3.5: Classifier cascade with n levels.

The advantage of using a cascade is that many image regions that do not show the object can be sorted out at the first levels with very low number of features, which results in low computation times. Viola and Jones showed that for the task of face detection, a classifier with only two features is able to detect 100% of all faces with a false positive rate of 40%. More difficult regions have to pass deeper in the cascade to be classified with a higher number of features. The overall detection rate D and the total false positive rate F of a cascade with N layers is

$$D = \prod_{i=1}^{N} d_i \qquad \text{and} \qquad F = \prod_{i=1}^{N} f_i \qquad (3.6)$$

where d_i is the detection rate and f_i the false positive rate of a single level i. To obtain a high total detection rate together with a low false positive rate, the detection rate of each single level should be kept high, while the false positive rate can be decreased by adding more levels. The training of a cascade is an optimization task, which includes the optimization of the number of cascade levels, the number of features at each level and the threshold for each strong classifier in order to minimize the total number of features that are used to achieve a given target detection rate D and false positive rate F. Viola and Jones proposed to solve this optimization problem in the following way: the user specifies the minimum rates f and d for each cascade level that are acceptable. After that, for each layer Adaboost is used to train a strong classifier until the given target rates f and d are met. The rates are determined using the classifier on a validation set. This way, more levels are added to the cascade until the overall false positive rate F is met. The algorithm for training a cascade is depicted in figure 3.4.3. The training is initialized with a set $\mathcal{P}$ of positive and a set $\mathcal{N}$ of negative training images, the maximum false positive rate f per layer, the minimum detection rate d per layer and the overall false positive rate F.

As one can see, the threshold of each strong classifier is decreased in an extra step after the Adaboost training in order to achieve the minimal detection rate. Decreasing the threshold results in a strong classifier with a higher detection rate at the expense of a higher false positive rate. This has to be done because Adaboost always minimizes the error rates.

procedure CascadeTraining($\mathcal{P}$, $\mathcal{N}$, F, f, d) : **returns** detector cascade
begin
    $F_0 := 1.0$; $D_0 := 1.0$; $i := 0$;
    while $F_i > F$ **do**
        $n_i := 0$; $F_i := F_{i-1}$; $i := i + 1$
        while $F_i > f \cdot F_{i-1}$ **do**
            $n_i := n_i + 1$;
            Train classifier with n_i features using Adaboost;
            Evaluate cascaded classifier and determine D_i and F_i;
            Decrease threshold θ_i for strong classifier i until $D_i \geq d \cdot D_{i-1}$;
        endwhile
        $\mathcal{N} := \emptyset$;
        if $F_i > F$ **then**
            Evaluate cascade on none-object images, put false detections into $\mathcal{N}$
        endif
    endwhile
end

Figure 3.6: Cascade training algorithm as proposed in [156].

Bootstrapping is applied to adjust the set of negative examples after training of each layer. Here, the cascade is used to classify a number of negative image examples and false positives are included in the set so that the next layer concentrates on these false positives that had not been classified correctly by the previous layer.

3.4.4 Applications and recent extensions

The work presented by Viola and Jones gained a lot of interest in the computer vision community and Adaboost has been used to learn classifiers for different kinds of object detection tasks. Since the approach has been originally proposed for face detection, most of the applications deal with this topic. However, the method has also been used to detect other types of objects and thus proofed the universality of the algorithm: Viola et al. used Adaboost to learn a classifier to detect pedestrians from a variety of different viewpoints [153]. In their work, the classifier combined the appearance features that were described above with motion features. Motion features are sum-of pixel differences on pairs of consecutive images in time and can also be calculated in integral images. The authors showed an improved detection performance of the dynamic detector that included motion over the static classifier. In their approach, additional runtime had to be spent on calculating a pyramid of difference images which was more than half of the total runtime of the system.

Nai et al. implemented the Adaboost detector for people detection in hardware on an FPGA (field programmable gate array) [98]. The system was designed to work together with a network camera as a standalone smart camera. The authors introduced an efficient algorithm for approximating the integral image from pictures that were JPEG coded and had to be decompressed. It was shown that the performance of the system was limited by the memory access time so that the creation and storage of an integral image of the size 216x288 that was created from an 352x288 image needed approximately 30ms. The frame rate for detection was specified with 2.5 frames per second on a MicroBlaze processor running at 75MHz.

Adaboost was also used for face and facial feature recognition. Littlewort et al. [89] used Adaboost to select Gabor filter features in order to classify and recognize seven different facial expressions with a SVM. Silapachote et al. in [128] compared Adaboost and SVM using histograms of Gabor and Gaussian derivate responses as features for facial expression recognition.

Jones and Viola learned a face similarity function to solve the face recognition task as shown in [69]. The similarity function compared two input images based on the sum of differences between a number of rectangular features. The Adaboost learning algorithm was extended in order to work with weak classifiers that operate on the difference of feature values in image pairs. A similar approach that introduced intra-face and extra-face differences in Gabor feature spaces can be found in [168] and [170].

Alternative methods for Boosting and cascade learning

Extensions to the Adaboost approach mainly deal with the implementation of alternative boosting methods and the improvement of the cascade learning algorithm. Alternative boosting methods that are used are e.g. FloatBoost [85], GentleBoost [13], Asymmetric Adaboost [154] or Kullback-Leibler Boosting [90]. In order to speed up the training of a cascaded detector, Wu et al. proposed a forward feature selection method that was used instead of Adaboost to learn a classifier node [161]. The main difference is that weak classifiers were trained only once per cascade level and not once for each feature.

Sun et al. [132] suggested to use different target detection and false positive rates for each level of the cascade. The target rates were adjusted based on a risk cost function which gives an optimal trade-off between the target rates given the desired false positive rate of the whole cascade.

A method called boosting chain learning was introduced by Xiao et al. in [165]. Here, a "chain" structure of subsequent classifier levels was introduced to utilize information from the previous stages. Instead of adjusting the threshold for each strong classifier to reach the given target rates, the authors suggest to learn optimized weights using a Support Vector Machine. Additionally, redundant weak classifiers were removed from each strong classifier using SVMs and Recursive Feature Elimination (see chapter 2) after each

Adaboost training. The boosting chain algorithm has also been used to detect faces from multiple views [164] and to locate facial features [29].

The soft cascade architecture that was proposed in [20] also allowed for information reuse of former classifier evaluations. The authors trained a single stage that can have a large number of weak classifiers. After each evaluation of the ith weak classifier, the cumulated total sum of all evaluations was compared to a rejection threshold r_i. If the cumulated sum was less than the threshold, the classification result was negative and otherwise the evaluation continued with the next weak classifier. A modified Adaboost algorithm that included bootstrapping was used to learn the weak classifiers and the authors described a method to compute the rejection thresholds and the ordering of the weak classifiers that minimized the false positive rate for a given target detection rate and target execution time.

Le and Satoh proposed the usage of two stages for object detection [81]. The first stage consisted of a cascade that was trained with Adaboost. Image regions that passed the first stage were classified with a nonlinear SVM (polynomial kernel) using pixel-features in a second stage. The authors showed that this method was slightly slower than a pure Adaboost cascade but the classification performance was slightly better. The same authors used a three-stage classifier in [82]. Here, the first two stages were cascaded classifiers that use different image resolutions (36x36 and 24x24) and the last stage was a SVM that uses 125 features from the last layer of the second cascade. The usage of Adaboost for feature selection and SVM for classification was also proposed by Le and Satoh in [80]. Here, Adaboost was used to preselect 200 features. From these sets, two subsets were created and the classification performance was compared using a SVM: the first subset consisted of the first 50 features in the order they were selected by Adaboost and a second subset of 50 features was created using a selection method based on PCA. The performance of the SVM classifier using the second subset was slightly better compared to the first subset.

Alternative methods for feature search

Only little work was done concerning the exhaustive search over all features and a feature set extension. Lilienhart et al. [86] showed that extending the basic feature set yields detectors with lower error rates. However, extending the feature set leads to much longer training times due to the exhaustive search over all possible features.

To reduce training time McCane et al. [93] proposed a simple heuristic search known as local search to find suboptimal features. However, they only used the base feature set with 4 different types of features and were only able to find classifiers that had slightly worse detection rates than those produced with exhaustive search.

Bartlett et al. [13] also used a heuristic to find promising features: After selecting 5% of all possible features randomly, they refined their selection by shifting, scaling and reflecting the best found features in small steps.

3.5 Summary

In this chapter current methods for detecting objects in images were described in detail. The description concentrated on approaches that learn a classifier offline using SVM and Adaboost and which can be processed online in real-time on standard PC hardware. The computational complexity of the classifiers that were learned with SVMs heavily depends on the number of support vectors, which can be very high without the usage of any method to approximate the support vectors. Second, most approaches for object detection with SVMs used a pixel-based object representation without any extra feature selection method. The rectangular features that were proposed by Viola and Jones can be calculated very quickly using the integral image representation. They can be rescaled without any computational effort while a pixel-based approach would require the computation of an image pyramid where the computational effort depends on the image resolution and the maximum scale at which an object shall be detected. Adaboost can be used to select a small number of discriminative features, while learning the classifier at the same time, so that no separate feature selection method is required. However, feature selection in Adaboost as proposed by Viola and Jones requires an exhaustive search over all features in each iteration of the algorithm so that the number of features has to be limited in advance. It was shown that increasing the feature set yields classifiers with higher performance but only little work was done in order to find alternative methods that are able to search in high dimensional feature spaces. Therefore, a new combination of Adaboost and Evolutionary Search is investigated in the next chapter.

Chapter 4

Optimizing Visual Object Detection

4.1 Introduction

This chapter addresses some of the disadvantages of the Adaboost method for object detection that was described in the last chapter. The main intention here is to develop methods to further improve classifiers concerning the classification performance and classification speed. The introduction of Adaboost to the problem of visual object detection has left some open questions which will be answered in this chapter:

- Does an extended set of features lead to higher classification performance?

- Can an extended set of features lead to classifiers with a lower total number of features?

- How can the exhaustive search in Adaboost be replaced by a heuristic search so that feature selection on an extended feature set is possible?

- Is there an alternative way to select features and design fast classifiers?

The first two questions deal with the exhaustive search over all possible features that is done in each iteration of Adaboost. Viola and Jones proposed the usage of only four different base types of rectangular features. An exhaustive search over all possible positions and scales of the features in all training images however requires a very high number of feature evaluations in each iteration of Adaboost. The total number of features that have to be searched explodes with the number of basic feature types and an exhaustive search cannot be performed within reasonable time. On the other hand, it has been shown that extended sets of features can improve the resulting classifiers [87].

This problem is solved in this chapter by introducing a heuristic search with an Evolutionary Algorithm which replaces the exhaustive search in each Adaboost iteration. This

new extension of Adaboost using EA is described in the first part of the chapter.
In the second part of the chapter an alternative method is proposed that does not need Adaboost for feature selection and classifier design. Adaboost can be seen as a "bottom-up" approach for feature selection because the algorithm adds promising features in a sequential way and evaluates only the classification error of the current weak classifier while the performance of the resulting strong classifier is not taken into account. This can lead to classifiers that use a high number of redundant features. A more "top-down" approach that directly operates on a set of strong classifiers using a combination of SVM and EA is developed in the second part of this chapter.

Parts of the work that is described in this chapter were published in [145].

4.2   Combining Adaboost with an Evolutionary Algorithm

In order to be able to search over an extended set of features, the exhaustive search over all features (step 3b in figure 3.4) is replaced by an Evolutionary Search (see figure 4.1).

```
procedure EAFeatureSearch(P) : returns P
begin
    t₂:=0;
    initialize_feature_population(P(0));
    repeat
        P' := select(P(t₂));
        crossover(P');
        mutate(P');
        train_classifiers(P');
        evaluate_classification_error(P');
        P(t₂ + 1) := replace(P(t₂), P');
        t₂ := t₂+1;
    until terminated;
end
```

Figure 4.1: Evolutionary Algorithm which replaces step 3b) in figure 3.4

We enlarge the base feature set, so that we come up with 6 different base types that are shown in figure 4.2. The weights w_i, $i = 1, ..., 4$ are integers between -4 and 4. The base features in [156] are special cases of our extended feature set. The first feature in figure 3.2, for example, is described by feature type $t = 3$ with $w_1 = 1$, $w_2 = -1$, $w_3 = -1$, $w_4 = 1$. We use these 6 base types to be comparable to [156] considering the

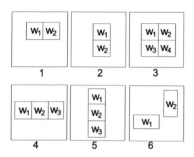

Figure 4.2: New feature set: 6 different geometrical layouts

runtime for calculating the feature response on an image. The most complex feature is the first one shown in figure 3.2 which requires 9 lookup operations in the integral image to calculate the result. None of the features in the extended set requires more than 9 lookup operations. The most general feature is feature number 6 in the new set (see figure 4.2). The two regions of interest can cover non symmetrical dependencies with larger spatial distance.

Every feature is encoded by a string of up to 13 integer variables (see figure 4.3):

- Base-type $k \in \{1, 2, ..., 6\}$ of the feature describing one of the six different geo-metrical layouts.

- Position (x_{tl}, y_{tl}) of the upper left corner within the detector subwindow

- Position (x_{br}, y_{br}) of the lower right corner within the detector subwindow

- Weights $w_i \in \{-4, ..., 4\}, i = 1, ..., 4$

- If $k = 6$: Upper left (x'_{tl}, y'_{tl}) and lower right (x'_{br}, y'_{br}) corner of second feature box

Therefore, the genotype of an individual is represented by the following 13-dimensional integer string: $(t, w_1, w_2, w_3, w_4, x_{tl}, y_{tl}, x_{br}, y_{br}, x'_{tl}, y'_{tl}, x'_{br}, y'_{br})$. With this representation, the problem of selecting features becomes a constrained non-linear integer programming problem. As a fitness function for evaluating individuals the error function $\epsilon_j = \sum_i w_{t,i} |h_j(x_i) - y_i|$ is used which is the same as in the original Adaboost training procedure. Therefore, to calculate the fitness of an individual j, we first evaluate the feature on every training example and determine the threshold θ_j to build a single weak classifier h_j. Fitness is then calculated as the mean classification error of the weak classifier on the training set. Individuals that are not suitable for building a classifier with low classification error will be penalized with a low fitness value and features that are highly discriminative will receive a high fitness value.

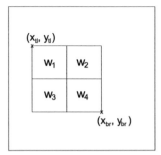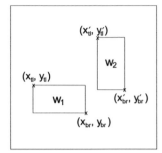

Figure 4.3: Parameters for features ($k = 3$ and $k = 6$)

The evolutionary search is driven by two main operators, crossover and mutation. Here, a standard uniform crossover is used. Given two parents A and B the resulting offspring C is calculated as follows:

$$C_i = \begin{cases} B_i & : & r \leq 0.5 \\ A_i & : & otherwise \end{cases} , i = 1...n \qquad (4.1)$$

where r is a uniform random number $\in [0, 1]$ and n describes the length of the individuals. Mutation of an individual is done by the following scheme:

1. Choose new type $t \in \{1, ..., 6\}$ with probability p_{mt}

2. Choose new weight with probability p_{mw}

3. Mutate positions of feature corners by adding a random constant (x_{rm}, y_{rm}), $x_{rm}, y_{rm} \in \{-3, ..3\}$

We use a repair operator on individuals that are no longer feasible after applying mutation and crossover. Individuals for which the upper left and lower right feature corners are in wrong order are repaired by altering corner positions. As the feature value has to be average free, the weights are rescaled by the repair operator so that they sum up to zero. In case of feature type $k = 6$, the repair operator also adjusts the sizes of the two regions of interest so that they are equal.

In the EA, parents are selected randomly and children replace the parent population with a standard $(\mu + \lambda)$ replacement.

4.2.1   Experiments

In the following the standard Adaboost learning with exhaustive search (ExBoost) is compared against the combination of Adaboost and evolutionary search, which will be called

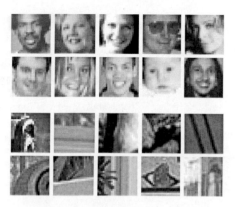

Figure 4.4: Images from face/non face set

Figure 4.5: Examples from the image set with balls/non balls

EABoost. ExBoost searches over the initial limited feature set, which is shown in figure 3.2, while EABoost applies the extended set of features. For training and testing two different image sets are used: One set containing faces and another set containing soccer balls. The face image set is provided by P. Carbonetto [27] and contains 4916 images showing different faces and 7872 images which do not show a face. Figure 4.4 shows some of the face and non face images. The face images seem to be the same as in the original experiments described by Viola and Jones. The gray value images have the size of 24x24 pixels and are variance normalized. The face/non face sets are split randomly into a training and a test set containing 2423 positive examples (faces) and 3737 negative examples (non faces) each. We sorted out those images from the original image set that were duplicate or too similar to others, because we do not want to have images in the test set that are too similar to the training set.

The second image set which is used in the experiments contains images showing a soccer ball (490 images per test/training set each) and randomly cropped picture regions where no ball is present at all (4145 images per test/training set each). The ball images have the size of 19x19 pixels. Figure 4.5 shows example images from the ball image set.

With both algorithms face and ball detectors were trained using the given training sets. Training was stopped when the resulting strong classifier labeled all examples in the training set correctly. Parameters used for evolution were: Population size $P = 250$, 20% of all individuals undergo crossover ($p_c = 0.2$), 80% of all individuals were mutated ($p_m = 0.8$) and the population was initialized randomly. In the following, averaged results over 20 runs of the EABoost experiments are shown. The EA terminated if the population was converged to a good solution so that no better individual was found within the next 50 generations. If convergence did not occur within 400 generations, the EA was stopped as well. All experiments were carried out on a Pentium III 650MHz processor.

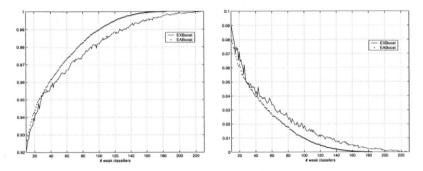

Figure 4.6: Classification rates (left) and false positive rates (right) on training set (face set)

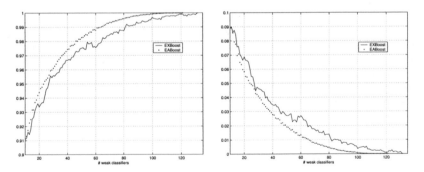

Figure 4.7: Classification rates (left) and false positive rates (right) on training set (ball set)

The classification rates and the false positive rates for both algorithms during training are shown in figure 4.6 and 4.7. For both training sets EABoost is able to find classifiers with a lower number of features compared to ExBoost. Table 4.1 shows the best, average and worst number of features. Note that the classifiers learned with EABoost use only 75%/82% (face set/ball set) of the number of features of ExBoost on average. Therefore, as shown in table 4.4, the classifiers can be evaluated faster.

Set	Algorithm	best	average	worst
Face set	ExBoost	227	227	227
Face set	EABoost	158	171	184
Ball set	ExBoost	132	132	132
Ball set	EABoost	99	108	121

Table 4.1: Number of selected features

Set	Algorithm	average time	average total time
Face set	ExBoost	185.2s	42040s
Face set	EABoost	63.5s	10868s
Ball set	ExBoost	57.8s	7627s
Ball set	EABoost	42.2s	4568s

Table 4.2: Training times

The results show, that training times are also reduced by the use of EABoost (see table 4.2). The mean time for the search for one weak classifier on the face set was 64 seconds for EABoost compared to 185 seconds for ExBoost which is a speedup of 2.9. In the ball set, we have smaller images, so that the search space is not as large as in the face set. In this case, training times for one iteration with EABoost are comparable to ExBoost. Note that the total training times for EABoost are much shorter due to the reduced iteration times and the reduced total number of classifiers.

The learned detectors were evaluated on the two test sets to compare detection and false positive rates (see figures 4.8 and 4.9). One can see that although the detectors that were learned with EABoost use a lower number of features, they are able to achieve higher detection rates with lower false positive rates on the test sets. For the face set, the best evolved detector (concerning detection rate on test set) uses only 163 features and classifies 96.9% of the face set correctly, compared to a classification rate of 96.1% achieved by the detector with 227 features found by ExBoost. On the set with ball images, the best evolved detector uses 119 features and classifies 98.3% of the set correctly, whereas the detector with 132 features found by ExBoost achieves a classification rate of 97.5%.

It is interesting to have a look at some of the features that EABoost evolved. Figure 4.10 shows the first six features that were selected for one of the strong classifiers by EABoost.

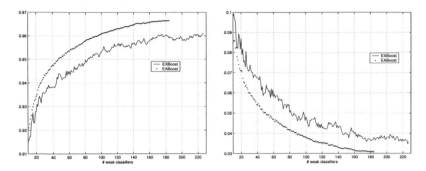

Figure 4.8: Classification rates (left) and false positive rates (right) on test set (face set)

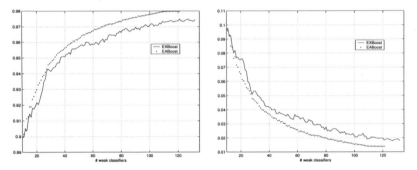

Figure 4.9: Classification rates (left) and false positive rates (right) on test set (ball set)

As one can see, the features mainly cover the regions around the eyes due to the fact that these regions are characteristic for faces. The newly proposed feature type with two unconnected regions can be found within the first significant features, too. This feature pays attention to the fact that mostly the area in the middle of the forehead (spotlight) is brighter than the area of the hair. Because those situations can better be handled by loosely coupled features, it is harder to find an appropriate classifier with one of the four base types with directly connected regions of interest.

Set	Algorithm	best	average	worst
Face set	ExBoost	96.1%	96.1%	96.1%
Face set	EABoost	96.9%	96.7%	96.4%
Ball set	ExBoost	97.5%	97.5%	97.5%
Ball set	EABoost	98.3%	98.0%	97.7%

Table 4.3: Classification rates on test sets

Set	Algorithm	best	average	worst
Face set	ExBoost	2.44s	2.44s	2.44s
Face set	EABoost	2.10s	2.28s	2.43s
Ball set	ExBoost	1.10s	1.10s	1.10s
Ball set	EABoost	0.98s	1.08s	1.19s

Table 4.4: Runtimes for final classifiers on complete test sets

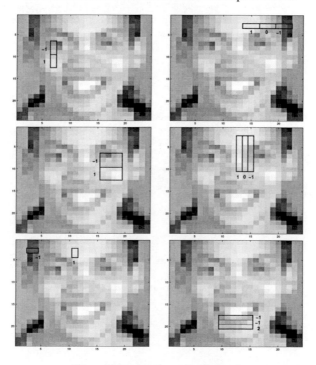

Figure 4.10: First six evolved features

4.3   Combining SVMs with an Evolutionary Algorithm

One disadvantage of using Adaboost for feature selection and classifier design is the iterative sequential way in which features are added to the final classifier. Only the local classification error of a single feature on the weighted training set is calculated, in order to choose the best weak classifier, while the total classification performance of the resulting strong classifier is not evaluated in each iteration. This can lead to the insertion of redundant features that increase the classification time while having no impact on the classification performance. Therefore, some authors proposed to remove features from the final strong classifier in an extra step (see [165]) which of course introduces extra effort in the training process. Therefore, an alternative "top-down" process that evaluates the performance of the whole classifier is proposed in this section.

The main idea is to use an Evolutionary Algorithm to search for a strong classifier that consists of a low number of features while achieving high classification performance. This means that each individual i in the population encodes a specific strong classifier with a different number of features m together with their weights w_j. Searching over a number of strong classifiers imposes two main problems: The EA has to deal with individuals that have different lengths (the number of features) and the values of the weights w_j for each weak classifier are unknown. The weights can of course also be encoded in the individual and optimized together with the number and types of features but this will lead to a high dimensional search space which is not necessary because the weights can directly be computed using a SVM. A linear SVM equals a strong classifier in the following way: Given a set of training examples $(\mathbf{z}_i, y_i)$ where $\mathbf{z}_i = [h_{1i}, h_{2i}, ..., h_{mi}]$ is a vector of the results of m weak classifiers h_{im} on the ith training image patch $\mathbf{x}_i$ and $y_i \in \{-1, 1\}$ specifies the class of the image patch, then the decision function $h(\mathbf{z})$ of a linear SVM for the unknown sample $\mathbf{z}$ is:

$$h(\mathbf{z}) = sgn\left(\sum_{i=1}^{l}\alpha_i y_i \langle \mathbf{z}, \mathbf{z_i}\rangle + b\right) \tag{4.2}$$

$$= sgn\left(\langle(\sum_{i=1}^{l}\alpha_i y_i \mathbf{z}_i), \mathbf{z}\rangle + b\right) \tag{4.3}$$

$$= sgn\left(\langle \mathbf{w}\mathbf{z}\rangle + b\right) \tag{4.4}$$

$$= sgn\left(\sum_{j=1}^{m} w_j h_j + b\right) \tag{4.5}$$

Note that in case of using a SVM the notation of a weak classifier h_j is slightly changed compared to section 3.4 so that $h_j(x) \in [-1; 1]$:

$$h_j(x) = \begin{cases} 1 & : \quad \text{if } p_j f_j(x) < p_j \theta_j \\ -1 & : \quad \text{otherwise} \end{cases} \tag{4.6}$$

where p_j, f_j and θ_j specify the parity, the feature and the threshold which are the same as in section 3.4. As one can see from equation 4.2, the training of a linear SVM yields the values for the weights w_j for each weak classifier h_j and the notation of the classifier is similar to a strong classifier with m weighted weak classifiers and a threshold b.

In order to use an Evolutionary Algorithm to optimize the feature set, each individual is encoded as a list of m different features. The features itself are rectangular features similar to the ones that were described in the last section with a similar encoding. The fitness of each individual (strong classifier) is then calculated in the following way: First, all features are evaluated on the training set and the thresholds θ_j for the related weak classifiers h_j are computed. Then, a linear SVM is trained in order to calculate the weights w_j. Finally, the strong classifier is evaluated on the training set to determine the classification rate c_r. The fitness of the individual i is then defined as

$$f(i) = \delta \cdot c_r(i) - m. \tag{4.7}$$

where δ denotes a constant factor and m is the number of features that are used in the strong classifier. Thus, the fitness function is designed to increase the classification rate while keeping a low number of features. A population of strong classifiers with different numbers of features is initialized randomly in the beginning. For each individual, a random number $m \in [1, max_m]$ of features is chosen and each feature is initialized randomly (random feature type and random position).

Problem specific crossover and mutation operators were designed in order to deal with individuals that have different lengths. The crossover operator takes two individuals a and b which consist of m_a and m_b features. In order to create a new individual c, a random number of features $m_c \in [m_a, m_b]$ is drawn uniformly first. All features $m \leq min(m_a, m_b)$ are generated by copying them alternately from the two parent individuals while the remaining features are copied directly from the individual with the higher number of features. In order to improve the crossover operator and include more problem specific knowledge, the features of a and b are sorted in descending order based on their weights w_i^2 first. A high value of w_j^2 is related to a high relevance of the feature (see section 2.3.5) so that the crossover creates an new classifier c that consists of the features from a and b that have the highest impact on the classification performance. Features in c that equal each other are finally removed. The proposed crossover operator that is based on feature ranking is depicted in figure 4.11.

Mutation of a strong classifier is done in two steps: First a random number $r \in [-10; 10]$ is used to compute a new total number of features $m_{new} = m + r$. If $m_{new} < m$ the last relevant features are deleted from the classifier, otherwise r new features are randomly initialized and added to the classifier. In a second step all features are mutated (mutation of position, scale etc., see previous section). The pseudo-code for mutation is given in figure 4.12.

```
procedure crossover(a, b) : returns c
begin
   relevance_sort(a); relevance_sort(b);
   m_a := length(a); m_b := length(b);
   if m_a > m_b then
      swap(a, b); swap(m_a, m_b);
   endif
   m_c := rnd(m_a, m_b);
   z_1 := 0; z_2 := 0;
   for k:= 1 to m_c do
      if z_1 <= m_a AND odd(k) then
         c_k := a_{z_1}; z_1 := z_1 + 1;
      else
         c_k := b_{z_2}; z_2 := z_2 + 1;
      endif
   endfor
   removeEqualFeatures(c);
end
```

Figure 4.11: Crossover operator for strong classifiers using feature ranking criterion.

```
procedure mutate(a) : returns a
begin
   relevance_sort(a);
   m := length(a);
   m' := m + rnd(-10, 10);
   for k:= m+1 to m' do
      initialize_feature(h_k);
   endfor
   for k:= 1 to m' do
      mutate_feature(h_k);
   endfor
   removeEqualFeatures(a);
end
```

Figure 4.12: Mutation operator for strong classifiers using feature ranking criterion.

4.3.1 Experiments

Parameters

The experiments were carried out on the image sets with faces and balls that were described in section 4.2.1. The parameters that were used for the Evolutionary Algorithm are depicted in table 4.5. A value of $C = 0.01$ was chosen for the linear SVM. The factor δ in the fitness function (see equation 4.7) was set to $\delta = 10^6$ so that the classification rate clearly controlled the fitness of the individuals. The number of features is usually less than 1000 and the values for classification rate lie between 0.5 and 1.0. With the chosen value of δ, the classification rate of an individual that consists of 100 features can be 0.01% worse than the rate of an individual with 200 features in order to get the same fitness value. The experiments were carried out on a Dual Core AMD Opteron processor with 2.4GHz. The results were averaged over 20 runs of each algorithm. The performance of the Evolutionary Algorithm that uses feature relevance recombination and mutation (EA_SVM1) and the EA that does not incorporate the feature ranking into the evolutionary operators (EA_SVM2) are compared in the following. In most cases, EA_SMV1 converged within 30 generations and EA_SVM_2 needed 80 generations so that the training was stopped for EA_SVM1 after 30 generations and for EA_SVM_2 after 80 generations.

Parameter	Value
Population size μ	80
Crossover rate p_c	0.4
Mutation rate p_m	0.6
Selection	random
Replacement	$(\mu + \lambda)$

Table 4.5: Parameters used in the experiments.

Algorithm comparison

The classification performance of EA_SVM1 and EA_SVM2 are compared in the following. The progress of the classification rates over the number of generations on the training set is shown in figure 4.13. The classification rate can be increased with a decreasing false positive rate with both algorithms. The final mean classification rate on the training set using EA_SVM1 was 97.9% (face set) and 99.0% (ball set). Compared to the Adaboost method which adds the features iteratively, classification rates of 100% cannot be obtained with the SVM. Both algorithms reduced the number of features during the evolution (see figure 4.14) and achieved a similar final number of classifiers on both image sets (see table 4.6).

Set	Algorithm	best	average	worst
Face set	EASVM_1	77	93	122
Face set	EASVM_2	75	93	109
Ball set	EASVM_1	73	89	112
Ball set	EASVM_2	80	93	113

Table 4.6: Number of selected features.

Set	Algorithm	best	average	worst
Face set	EASVM_1	96.7%	96.3%	95.9%
Face set	EASVM_2	95.5%	95.1%	94.8%
Ball set	EASVM_1	97.9%	97.7%	97.5%
Ball set	EASVM_2	97.2%	96.9%	96.2%

Table 4.7: Classification rates on test sets.

The classification and false positive rates on the test sets are shown in figure 4.15. The classification rates of the classifiers that were evolved with both algorithms increased during the evolution while the false positive rates decreased. On both test sets EA_SVM1 performed better than EA_SVM2. Table 4.7 compares the classification rates on the test sets for the final classifiers. On both test sets, the mean classification rates using EA_SVM1 were higher compared to EA_SVM2. The best classifier concerning the classification rate on the face set was evolved using EA_SVM1 and consisted of 91 features with a classification rate of 96.7%. The best classifier for the ball set had 88 features and a classification rate of 97.9%. With these results, EA_SVM1 also outperformed the standard Adaboost algorithm.

The time that was needed for the evolved classifiers to classify the whole test sets are depicted in table 4.8. The mean time for the evaluation of one generation of EA_SVM1 was 343s (face set) and 146s (ball set) while EA_SMV2 needed 487s (face set) and 210s (ball set). Another advantage of EA_SVM1 was the faster convergence of the algorithm so that with this approach the training time was decreased substantially.

Set	Algorithm	best	average	worst
Face set	EASVM_1	81.5ms	103.9ms	133.1ms
Face set	EASVM_2	86.1ms	101.7ms	122.5ms
Ball set	EASVM_1	56.7ms	73.1ms	91.5ms
Ball set	EASVM_2	64.7ms	75.1ms	90.0ms

Table 4.8: Classification times on test sets.

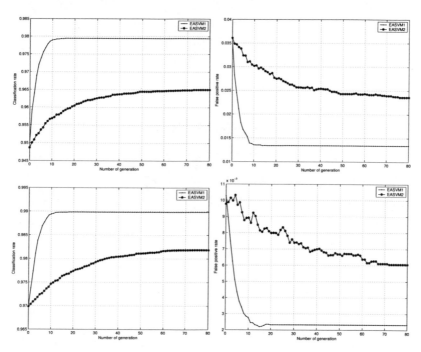

Figure 4.13: Classification rates (left) and false positive rates (right) on training sets (top: face set, bottom: ball set)

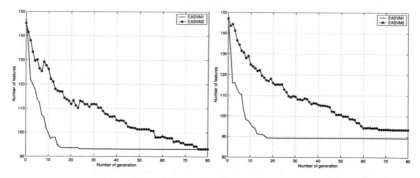

Figure 4.14: Number of features over number of generations (left: face set, right: ball set)

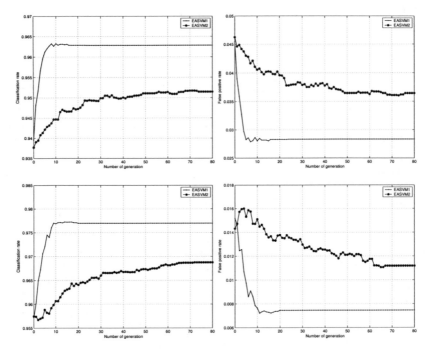

Figure 4.15: Classification rates (left) and false positive rates (right) on training sets (top: face set, bottom: ball set)

4.4   Related Work

The use of Evolutionary Algorithms in the field of image processing, especially automatic selection of features and learning classifiers for object detection, is a field of research which receives growing interest. Most of the publications use either a Genetic Algorithm for feature selection or Genetic Programming in order to evolve visual routines. The method proposed by Sun et. al [134] is conceptually closest to the SVM_EA approach that was presented in the second part of this chapter. The authors encoded a number of Gabor filters in bit strings and optimized these features using a Genetic Algorithm. Object classification was done using a nonlinear SVM. The main differences to the combination of EA and SVM in this chapter were

- Different types of features, Gabor filters are not runtime optimized.

- Use of standard crossover and mutation techniques instead of special operators using feature ranking.

- Nonlinear SVM with a higher runtime compared to the linear SVM employed here.

In [133], the same authors used a GA to select a number of eigenvectors that were used as features in SVM classification. Here, the maximal number of features was comparatively low (max. 200), so that a bit string encoding could be used where each bit was set if the associated feature was included in the classifier. Standard crossover and mutation techniques were used in this approach to modify individuals.

Howard et al. [65] applied Genetic Programming (GP) to build a classifier that detects ships in satellite images. Krawiec [77] extended standard GP by a local search operation for visual learning. Lin et al. [88] proposed a co-evolutionary GP to learn composite features based on primitive features that were designed by human experts. Bala et al. [11] combined a Genetic Algorithm (GA) with decision tree learning: The GA selected a good subset of features from a fixed set and a decision tree was learned to build the detector structure. Guarda et al. [54] combined a GA to select different convolution masks (features) with GP to evolve the final detector based on logical combinations of pixel convolutions in subwindows.

4.5   Summary

This chapter addressed some open questions and problems in using the standard Adaboost for the training of fast image classifiers. The first problem was the exhaustive search over all features that is done in each iteration of Adaboost in order to find a weak classifier with lowest training error. A new extension using Evolutionary Search in each iteration was developed in the first part of the chapter. With this extension it was possible to increase the set of features while being able to search this set in reasonable time. Compared to the standard Adaboost algorithm it was possible to train classifiers that have higher classification rates and use a lower number of features. The training time was also reduced.

Another disadvantage of using Adaboost is the iterative way in which features are added to form the final strong classifier. In the second part of this chapter it was shown how classifiers can be trained using an Evolutionary Algorithm that optimizes a population of strong classifiers directly. A linear Support Vector Machine was used to calculate the weights of the weak classifiers and the Evolutionary Algorithm searched for an optimal subset of features. New crossover and mutation operators were developed that were able to deal with individuals that have different lengths. The new operators use a feature ranking criterion to produce new individuals that consist of only the most relevant features. The experiments showed that the new approaches were able to outperform the mutation and crossover operators that do not apply the feature ranking criterion.

The algorithms that were developed in this chapter improve the training and the classification performance of a single strong classifier. Cascade learning was not addressed in this chapter but all proposed methods can be easily integrated into the known approaches for cascade learning.

Chapter 5

Tracking Objects in Image Sequences

5.1 Introduction

This chapter deals with algorithms to track objects in image sequences. If a target object is detected in a single image using strategies that have been described in the previous chapters, object tracking is used to update and predict the location of this object in the next frame of an image sequence. Tracking allows for a reduction of the time complexity since the scanning of each image at every position and scale is not necessary and the expensive evaluation of a classifier can be reduced to certain sample positions that are predicted using the information from the last time step. In the first part of this chapter, the problem of object tracking is introduced formally. After that, two algorithms, Kalman filtering and Condensation or Particle filtering, which are a well known solutions to the tracking problem, are described in more detail. The main focus lies on the Condensation algorithm due to its ability to achieve robust tracking of nonlinear motion in cluttered environments. Due to these properties, Condensation has been used to address a lot of different tracking problems. A main constraint for real time application of the Condensation algorithm is the high number of expensive image measurements that is needed for robust tracking. This chapter addresses the problem and describes extensions to Condensation that had been developed over the last years in literature. The chapter concludes with a description of techniques for tracking multiple objects.

5.2 The Tracking Problem

Visual object tracking is the process of determining a certain object configuration in an image sequence over time. The object configuration can be multidimensional and may consist of e.g. position, size, orientation and 3D-pose of the target object. The different tracking techniques usually include four basic elements that characterize the tracking performance (see also [163]): target representation, observation representation, hypothesis generation and hypothesis measurement. The target representation characterizes the target that has to be tracked and discriminates the target from other objects. A target in image sequences can be represented e.g. by shape, geometry, motion, color or gray level appearance. Closely related to the target representation is the observation representation which defines the kind of image features that are used to observe a certain target representation. An object that is represented, for example, by a certain contour or shape template can be observed in the image using edges and gradients in gray values that represent the object contour. The measurement of hypothesis relates the target observation to the target representation and can be defined as a fitness or likelihood function that measures the probability of a match between a hypothesis and the observation in the image. Generating hypotheses is the way of calculating new state predictions based on former estimates and observations. This process includes the description of the target dynamics that are modeled to predict possible object states.

The tracking problem can be formulated in a probabilistic framework as follows: Given a number of image observations $Z_t = \{\mathbf{z_t}, \mathbf{z_{t-1}}, ..., \mathbf{z_0}\}$ with actual measurement $\mathbf{z_t}$ and past observations $\mathbf{z_{t-1}}, ..., \mathbf{z_0}$, one has to find the actual object state $\mathbf{x_t}$ that maximizes $p_t(\mathbf{x_t}|Z_t)$. Applying Bayes' theorem at each time step, the posterior p_t can be calculated as:

$$p_t(\mathbf{x_t}|Z_t) = \frac{p_t(Z_t|\mathbf{x_t})p_{t-1}(\mathbf{x_t}|Z_{t-1})}{p_t(Z_t)}. \tag{5.1}$$

The object dynamics can be modeled as a Markov-process with a conditional probability $p_t(\mathbf{x_t}|\mathbf{x_{t-1}})$ so that equation 5.1 becomes

$$p_t(\mathbf{x_t}|Z_t) = \frac{p_t(Z_t|\mathbf{x_t}) \int_{x_{t-1}} p_t(\mathbf{x_t}|\mathbf{x_{t-1}})p_{t-1}(\mathbf{x_{t-1}}|Z_{t-1})d\mathbf{x_{t-1}}}{p_t(Z_t)}. \tag{5.2}$$

In general, this equation cannot be solved analytically without any restrictions. Well-known and widely-used solutions to the tracking problem are Kalman Filters [70] and Particle Filters [39]. In Kalman filtering, the observation density $p_t(Z_t|\mathbf{x_t})$ is assumed to be Gaussian distributed and the object dynamics have to be linear with Gaussian noise. In this case there exists a close solution for equation 5.2 (see section 5.3). Extended Kalman filters have been proposed to deal with nonlinear dynamics but the assumption of Gaussian distributed noise and observation density still remains. Particle Filters which apply the concept of Monte Carlo simulation do not underlie those restrictions and in the area of Computer Vision Isard and Blake adopted the idea of Particle Filtering to introduce the well known Condensation algorithm [66] which will be described in section 5.4.

5.3 Kalman Filter

R.E. Kalman published in 1960 [70] a recursive solution to the filtering problem to determine the estimate $\hat{\mathbf{x}}_t$ of an unknown object state $\mathbf{x}_t$ which evolves in a linear time discrete process. The notation that is used to describe the filtering process in the following is oriented to the descriptions in [158]. In a Kalman filter, the actual observation $\mathbf{z}_t$ is related to the object state by

$$\mathbf{z}_t = H\mathbf{x}_t + \mathbf{v}_t. \tag{5.3}$$

The state is mapped to the measurement by the matrix H with measurement noise $\mathbf{v}_t \sim N(0, R)$ and measurement noise covariance R.

The recursive Kalman filter algorithm consists of two steps, which are the time update or prediction step followed by a measurement update or correction step. In the first step, the object state estimate $\hat{\mathbf{x}}_{t-1}$ is predicted using

$$\hat{\mathbf{x}}_t' = A\hat{\mathbf{x}}_{t-1} + B\mathbf{u}_{t-1}. \tag{5.4}$$

Here, the matrix A maps the previous state at time $t - 1$ to the state at time t and the optional control vector $\mathbf{u}_{t-1}$ is related to the state via the matrix B. The error covariance P_{t-1} of the estimation is also predicted by

$$P_t' = AP_{t-1}A^T + Q \tag{5.5}$$

with the process noise covariance matrix Q.

The prediction step is followed by a measurement step which starts with the computation of the Kalman gain matrix K_t:

$$K_t = P_t'H^T(HP_t'H^T + R)^{-1}. \tag{5.6}$$

The Kalman gain minimizes the a posteriori error covariance (see [70] for more details). After computing the Kalman gain, the new state estimate $\hat{\mathbf{x}}_t$ can be calculated by incorporation of the actual measurement $\mathbf{z}_t$:

$$\hat{\mathbf{x}}_t = \hat{\mathbf{x}}_t' + K_t(\mathbf{z}_t - H\hat{\mathbf{x}}_t') \tag{5.7}$$

The difference $(\mathbf{z}_t - H\hat{\mathbf{x}}_t')$ between the actual measurement $\mathbf{z}_t$ and the predicted estimate $H\hat{\mathbf{x}}_t'$ is called innovation or residual $\mathbf{r}_t$. The innovation is weighted with the Kalman gain K_t to correct the estimate $\hat{\mathbf{x}}_t'$. In case that the covariance R of the measurement error converges to zero, the innovation gets a higher weight due to the fact that

$$\lim_{R_t \to 0} K_t = H^{-1}. \tag{5.8}$$

The innovation is weighted less heavily if the estimation error covariance P_t' gets close to zero:

$$\lim_{P_t' \to 0} K_t = 0. \tag{5.9}$$

Finally the a posteriori error covariance estimate is computed using

$$P_t = (I - K_t H) P_t'. \tag{5.10}$$

The recursive way of time update and measurement update in the Kalman filter that has been described above is outlined in figure 5.1. The prediction of the estimate $\hat{x}_{t-1}$ is depicted in the right part of the diagram. The left part shows the update step, which consists of the calculation of the residual r_t which is weighted with the Kalman gain in order to compute the new state estimation $\hat{x}_t$.

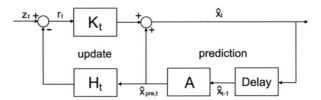

Figure 5.1: Kalman filter block diagram.

5.4   The Condensation algorithm

The Condensation algorithm had been proposed by Isard and Blake [66] and is a so called Sequential Importance Resampling (SIR) Filter which belongs to the class of Particle Filters [39] . The main idea of Condensation is to approximate the probability $p_t(\mathbf{x}_t|Z_t)$ of observing the object state $\mathbf{x}_t$ given the measurements Z_t by a set of N weighted samples:

$$S_t = \{\mathbf{x}_t^{(i)}, \pi_t^{(i)}\}, \ i = 1...N. \tag{5.11}$$

Each $\mathbf{x}_t^{(i)}$ describes a possible state weighted with $\pi_t^{(i)}$ which is proportional to the likelihood that the object is observed in this state. The Condensation algorithm consists of three main steps:

1. Create a new sample set S_t by resampling from the old sample set S_{t-1} based on the sample weights $\pi_{t-1}^{(i)}, i = 1...N$.

2. Predict sample states based on the dynamic model $p(\mathbf{x}_t^{(i)}|\mathbf{x}_{t-1}^{(i)}), i = 1...N$.

3. Calculate new weights by application of the measurement model:
   $\pi_t^{(i)} \propto p(\mathbf{z}_t|X_t = \mathbf{x}_t^{(i)}), i = 1...N$. Normalize the weights so that $\sum_{i=1}^N \pi_t^{(i)} = 1$.

The estimate of the object state at time t is the weighted mean over all sample states:

$$\hat{X}_t = E(S_t) = \sum_{i=1}^{N} \pi_t^{(i)} \mathbf{x}_t^{(i)}. \tag{5.12}$$

Figure 5.2 shows the prediction of the one dimensional probability function in one iteration of the algorithm.

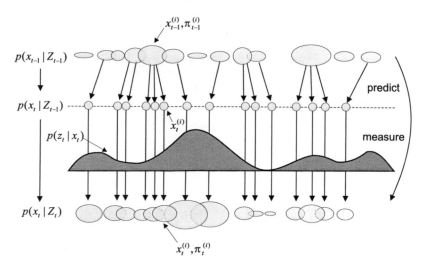

Figure 5.2: Probability density propagation using the Condensation algorithm (see [66]).

The resampling step to create a new sample set based on the previous set is done by calculation of cumulative weights $c_t^{(i)}$ that are stored together with each sample i. After the application of the measurement model and the computation of the weights $\pi_t^{(i)}$, the cumulative weights $c_t^{(i)}$ are calculated as:

$$c_t^{(0)} = 0, \tag{5.13}$$
$$c_t^{(i)} = c_t^{(i-1)} + \pi_t^{(i)}, \ i = 1, ..., N. \tag{5.14}$$

A sample $\mathbf{x}_t^{(i)}$ in the resampling step is then selected as follows:

- Generate a uniformly distributed random number $r \in [0, 1]$.

- Find the smallest index j for which $c_{t-1}^{(j)} \geq r$.

- Set $\mathbf{x}_t^{(i)} = \mathbf{x}_{t-1}^{(j)}$.

Resampling in this way guarantees that samples with higher weights are selected more often (proportional to their weight) than samples with lower weights. In the field of Evolutionary Algorithms this method equals a roulette-wheel selection (see chapter 2).

The measurement model relates the observation to the target representation and defines the likelihood of observing the image configuration $\mathbf{z}_t$ given a certain object state $\mathbf{x}_t$. A number of different observation models have been studied in the literature e.g.:

- Contour models [66]: Objects are modeled with spline contours and the likelihood function is calculated based on edge detection along the spline. The better a certain configuration of edges fits to the contour spline that is described by the particle the higher is the likelihood for this observation.

- Color models [107], [101]: The color distribution (e.g. histogram) of a template object is compared to the color information in the region that is described by each sample.

- Gray level features [84]: An offline learned classifier that uses features in gray images is evaluated at the position of each sample.

The dynamics $p(\mathbf{x}_t|\mathbf{x}_{t-1})$ of the target object can be modeled e.g. by a first order process:

$$\mathbf{x}_t = A\mathbf{x}_{t-1} \cdot B\mathbf{w}_t, \ \mathbf{w}_t \sim N(0,1) \tag{5.15}$$

where $B\mathbf{w}_t$ describes the process noise (stochastic drift) and A represents the deterministic component of the dynamics. Values for A and B can be determined experimentally or learned offline on training sequences (see e.g. [17]).
The Condensation algorithm that iterates over resampling, prediction and measurement based on observation likelihood is shown in figure 5.4.

The samples in Condensation are usually initialized randomly in order to cover the whole state space. Initialization and propagation of the samples in case of tracking a soccer ball is shown exemplarily in figure 5.4. Here, the state of each sample is three-dimensional and describes a quadratic area in the image that contains a soccer ball. As one can see in the figure, the samples are initialized randomly in the first image and after two iterations of the Condensation algorithm the samples gather around the true object position. The measurement model in this example evaluates a strong classifier that had been learned off line using Adaboost (see chapter 3). More details on the implementation of measurement models based on gray features and color distributions are given in the next chapter.

Condensation is able to achieve robust tracking results in cluttered environments or in situations where the target object is temporarily occluded (see figure 5.5). A comparison between Kalman filtering and Condensation on the problem of tracking object contours in

```
procedure Condensation(S): returns S
begin
    t:=0;
    initialize(S₀);
    evaluate(S₀);
    repeat
        S_{t+1}={};
        for i := 1 to N do
            x_t^(i):=select(S_t);
            x_{t+1}^(i):=drift(x_t^(i));
            π_{t+1}^(i):=evaluate(x_{t+1}^(i));
            S_{t+1}:=S_{t+1} ∪ {(x_{t+1}^(i), π_{t+1}^(i))}
        endfor
        t:=t+1;
    until termination;
end
```

Figure 5.3: Condensation algorithm.

images is e.g. given in [17] and shows the better performance of Condensation on difficult test sequences. The robustness comes mainly from the fact that multiple hypotheses are generated and tested. The tracking accuracy can be increased by increasing the number of samples but high dimensional state-spaces require an exponential increase in the number of hypotheses. MacCormick and Blake showed in [92] that the number of particles N that are needed for robust tracking can be calculated using a survival diagnostic $\mathcal{D}$ and a survival rate α. The survival diagnostic is also called estimated effective sample rate and is defined as

$$\mathcal{D} = \left(\sum_{i=1}^{N} \pi_i^2 \right)^{-1} \tag{5.16}$$

The value of $\mathcal{D}$ can be thought of as the number of particles that will "survive" the re-sampling step: if only one weight has the value $\pi_1 = 1$ and all others are set to zero then always the same particle is chosen for the next time step ($\mathcal{D} = 1$). If on the other hand all weights are equal ($\pi = \frac{1}{N}$) then each sample will be chosen once ($\mathcal{D} = N$). Thus, the survival diagnostic can be used to specify the tracking performance. Low values of $\mathcal{D}$ indicate that the final state estimate may be unreliable and the target could be lost due to the fact that it is only covered by a low number of particles. Given the prior distribution $p_{t-1}(x)$ and the posterior $p_t(x)$, which are represented by the particle set, the survival rate α is given by

$$\alpha = \left(\int p_t(x)^2 / p_{t-1}(x) dx \right)^{-1}. \tag{5.17}$$

If one fixes a minimum survival diagnostic $\mathcal{D}_{min}$ that is acceptable for robust tracking then the number of particles that are needed can be estimated as

$$N \geq \frac{\mathcal{D}_{min}}{\alpha^d}. \tag{5.18}$$

where d is the dimension of the state space and $\alpha \ll 1$ is a constant problem depending value. From this equation one can see that N increases linearly with the minimal expected survival rate and exponentially with the dimension of the state space. However the evaluation of a high number of samples in images introduces high computational costs. Thus, several methods for efficient tracking with a reduced number of samples have been proposed in the past and will be described in the following sections.

Figure 5.4: Condensation tracking: Initialization and propagation of samples (20% of all samples with the highest measurement likelihood).

Figure 5.5: Condensation tracking under occlusion.

5.4.1 Mixed-State Condensation

An exact modeling of the object dynamics can be used to decrease the number of particles that are needed for robust tracking. Instead of modeling the motion of the target object with one single dynamic model, Isard and Blake proposed in [68] a mixed-state Condensation tracker that allows for multiple motion models. Here, the state $x_t^{(i)}$ is extended by a discrete variable $y_t^{(i)} \in \{1, ..., N_m\}$ that labels a specific motion model out of N_m predefined models. The prediction is then extended in two steps: first, a motion model is selected by assigning y_t^i based on a transition probability matrix T, where T_{kl} specifies the probability of switching to motion model l while the actual model index is k. After that, the prediction of the sample is done according to the selected dynamic model. Isard and Blake used the mixed-state tracker to track a bouncing ball with 2 different models (constant acceleration model and "bounce" model). They also used a three-state model to follow a hand that draws with a pen (a general line drawing motion, a "scribbling" motion and a stationary state). Mixed-state Condensation can be applied in situations where different dynamics can be identified and modeled. The transition matrix T is usually specified by hand. However, in a real-world scenario it could be impossible to extract different motion models and define the transition probabilities (e.g. tracking randomly moving objects from a moving robot) so that motion can only be modeled very poorly with a high amount of random noise.

5.4.2 ICondensation

In standard Condensation, the positions of samples in the state-space only depend on the previous estimate at time $t - 1$ and the dynamic model. If the number of samples is large enough so that the state-space is covered sufficiently robust tracking even when the target moves with sudden changes in motion can be ensured. Decreasing the number of samples in order to decrease the run time of the algorithm increases the probability of loosing the track. Without any additional information large areas of the state-space do not contain any samples so that the robustness of the tracker is decreased. To be able to include additional measurements with a lower number of samples, Isard and Blake proposed the usage of importance sampling to extend the standard Condensation algorithm (Importance Condensation or ICondensation, [67]). ICondensation can be applied when auxiliary information about the state-space is available in form of an importance function $g(X)$. This can be any kind of function to measure visual attention over the whole image (optical flow, color distribution, etc.). The idea is then to position some of the samples in regions where the importance function provides high measurement probabilities instead of resampling from the previous density at time $t - 1$. This is done by modifying the resampling and measurement process for each sample i in the following way:

1. Choose a sampling method by the generation of the random number $\alpha \in [0, 1)$ and sample as follows:

   (a) If $\alpha \geq q+r$ use standard Condensation sampling based on cumulative weights. Set $\lambda_t^{(i)} = 1$.

(b) If $q \leq \alpha \leq q + r$ use importance sampling from $g(X_t)$ and calculate the correction term $\lambda_t^{(i)}$.

(c) If $\alpha < q$ use initialization and set $\lambda_t^{(i)} = 1$.

2. Measure and calculate weights using the correction term:
$\pi_t^{(i)} = \lambda_t^{(i)} p(z_t | X_t = x_t^{(i)})$.

Here, the constants q and r define the probabilities for the three different sampling methods: Importance sampling is done with probability r, samples are initialized with probability q and standard sampling is used with probability $1 - q - r$. A correction term $\lambda_t^{(i)}$ is used to adapt the likelihood in case of importance sampling. This is necessary to keep information about motion coherence so that a correct probability distribution can be calculated (for more details on the calculation of $\lambda_t^{(i)}$ see [67]. In situations where no additional information can be measured or the time for obtaining such information is too high for real-time tracking, ICondensation cannot be used.

5.4.3   Partitioned Sampling

Partitioned sampling ([91] [92]) had been introduced to deal with high-dimensional search spaces which occur in multi-object tracking (see section 5.5) or tracking of articulated objects that consists of different parts. The main idea of partitioned sampling is to divide the state-space into different partitions and then apply the dynamics and weighting function sequentially for each partition. This technique implies that independent dynamics and weighting functions exist for each partition, which means that it assumes that it is possible to independently localize different parts of an articulated object in case of single object tracking.

5.4.4   Annealed Particle Filter

Deutscher et al. proposed the usage of an Annealed Particle Filter [37] for tracking in high-dimensional state spaces to avoid the assumptions that are made in Partitioned Sampling. In Annealed Particle filtering, which is inspired by Simulated Annealing [74], each prediction and weighting step is done in a number of m layers. For each layer a weighting function w_m has to be defined in a way that w_m differs only slightly from w_{m-1} and w_M is designed to approximate the "true" state probability only roughly, while w_0 is very specific and covers local maxima. Starting with layer M, in each layer m the particles are weighted using w_m and after that they are resampled equal to this weighting to select samples that are then used to initialize the population for the next layer $m-1$. After m iterations all samples should be located in local maxima of the high-dimensional state-space. Deutscher et al. showed improved tracking performance over standard Condensation in tracking human body configurations for motion capturing.

5.4.5   Auxiliary Particle Filter

In situations where the dynamics of a target cannot be modeled very accurately the probability that Condensation places samples in "wrong" regions of the state-space can be very high. In this case it would be better to resample from the actual observation distribution rather than from the prior. In [105] Pitt and Shepard introduced an Auxiliary Particle Filter (APF) where the prediction of samples is done in two steps. First, for each particle i a position $\mu_t^{(i)}$ is determined which is a value that is likely to be generated from the dynamic model. A weight π is computed. In the second step, resampling is done based on the actual weights instead of the values from the last time step $t - 1$. Compared to standard Condensation, the Auxiliary Particle Filter requires two evaluations of the measurement model per particle with high computational costs. However, it is expected that the total number of particles can be decreased due to more efficient sampling based on the current observation.

5.4.6   Iterated likelihood weighting

Charif et al. compared standard Condensation, Auxiliary Particle Filter and their method which is called iterated likelihood weighting (ILW) [99]. In this comparison, ILW yields the best tracking performance followed by APF and Condensation with the poorest performance. In ILW, the set of samples is split into 2 equal parts after the resampling step. One part is resampled and measured on the actual image over a number of iterations in order to move the samples to regions with higher measurement probabilities. This iterative search is closely related to Local Search Particle Filters which are described in the next section. The disadvantage of ILW is that this method requires $\frac{N}{2} \cdot k$ additional measurement evaluations over a number of k iterations with a total number of N particles. However, the total number of particles can be reduced so that ILW is able to achieve better performance using the same number of evaluations compared to standard Condensation.

5.4.7   Local Search Particle Filter

Torma et al. proposed in [139] and [138] an extended Particle Filter that uses a local search operator to predict the state of each sample for the next time step. This operator is used to refine the predictions that come from the dynamic model in order to find better particle positions in the vicinity of each prediction. The design of this extra operator depends on the type of hypotheses representation and extra runtime has to be spent on processing the search. The authors showed that robust tracking of shape contours in images is possible using a local search operator that searches for maximal edge likelihoods in the vicinity of the predicted measurement points. Here, most of the runtime is spent on calculating image observations and evaluating the local search so that the runtime of their algorithm is twice as high as in standard Particle filtering with the same number of particles.

5.5   Tracking multiple objects with Condensation

The Condensation algorithm is theoretically able to maintain multiple hypotheses in a multi-modal probability distribution and therefore, tracking of multiple objects at the same time is possible. However, in practical applications one usually recognizes a so called sample impoverishment which means that after some time steps all samples tend to cover the regions in the image which have the highest observation probability so that the track of other targets that are visible under conditions which produce lower observation probabilities (overlap, illumination, etc.) is lost. In the literature one can find different extensions for Particle filters in order to deal with multiple objects. In principle one can distinguish between two different approaches: separated filters for each target and one single high-dimensional filter for all targets.

In methods that use a single filter for all objects each sample includes the configuration of all target objects ([91],[130]). In this case, the dimension of the state space is extremely high and increases with the number of objects. The maximal number of objects that can be tracked is fixed and has to be known in advance. The advantage of a single filter for all object configurations is that interactions between different targets can be modeled properly.

In order to avoid high-dimensional search spaces one can use a single filter per object ([148], [152], [102]). These approaches usually include a clustering step to identify different groups of samples in the configuration space. Samples in each cluster are then evaluated and predicted with a separated filter iteration. Special attention has to be paid in case of interaction between objects to maintain unambiguous assignment of samples that estimate the state of one particular object to a single cluster. Especially in situations where objects are close to each other or overlap, it can be difficult to separate the samples into different clusters and maintain the separation over time. The advantage of using a single filter for each object is that the number of possible objects must not be known in advance and can change over time.

5.6   Summary

After a formal introduction into the problem of tracking objects in image sequences, this chapter focused mainly on the Condensation algorithm which offers a number of advantages like e.g.

- Ability to deal with multi-modal and non-Gaussian state spaces.

- Robustness due to generation of multiple hypotheses.

- Dependence of the runtime on the number of samples which can be adjusted to a given environment.

- Easy implementation of the basic algorithm. Problem specific knowledge has only to be incorporated into the measurement and the dynamic model.

The number of particles and thus the number of image measurements that are needed for robust tracking increases exponentially with the dimension of the state space. In order to reduce the number of samples, different extensions to the Condensation algorithm have been presented. However, all of the extensions that have been described in this chapter need either extra likelihood evaluations, which are expensive image processing operations, or the definition of an extra function (local search or importance function) that has to be evaluated with extra costs. Although the total number of samples can be reduced or better performance with the same number of evaluations can be achieved by those methods, it should be possible to use information that is already contained in the population of particles to improve tracking performance without the need for extra evaluations and functions. The usage of internal population information (diversity, best individual, crossover between selected individuals) plays an important role in population based heuristic optimization algorithms like e.g. Evolutionary Algorithms (see chapter 2). Evolutionary Algorithms and Particle Filters share a lot of similarities which will be highlighted in the next chapter. Here, different extensions to the Condensation algorithm using methods that come from the field of heuristic optimization are proposed to reduce the number of particles while improving the tracking performance.

Chapter 6

Condensation Tracking and Heuristic Optimization

6.1 Introduction

In practical tracking applications, the evaluation of the measurement model, which has to be done for each sample, is the most time consuming part of the algorithm. The processing time can be effectively reduced by decreasing the total number of samples. On the other hand, reducing the number of samples can lead to poor tracking accuracy due to the fact that the state-space is no longer covered sufficiently. Therefore, one is interested in new ideas that can be incorporated into the tracking algorithm to be able to reduce the number of samples while keeping the robustness of the tracker. In this chapter, several extensions to the Condensation algorithm are proposed that exploit the similarities between Condensation and heuristic optimization techniques like Evolutionary Algorithms and Particle Swarms. These similarities are highlighted in the first section. After that, a Condensation algorithm that uses crossover operators and Condensation using Particle Swarm dynamics are introduced. Here, the main goal is to develop tracking algorithms that do not need expensive extra iterations or an extra measurement function but exploit information that is implicitly contained in the population of samples. This is especially important in real-time scenarios where only a low number of samples can be evaluated. The algorithms are analyzed and compared using different numbers of samples and different test sequences for visual tracking in an unconstrained environment and in front of a cluttered background. All experiments are carried out with a very general motion model which is often applied in order to track a randomly moving object from a moving observer. Especially in this case were no exact motion model is available, the tracking accuracy with standard Condensation can be low due to the fact that the samples are not correctly positioned using the motion model alone.

6.2 Condensation and Evolutionary Algorithms

The similarity of Condensation or Particle Filters in general and Evolutionary Algorithms was pointed out by some authors in the past (see section 6.4). Both methods use a discrete set of potential solutions (population of individuals in EA, particles or sample set in Condensation) that are propagated iteratively using the principle of survival-of-the fittest based on a fitness value or weight. The fitness value in EAs is usually time independent (except for dynamic optimization problems as e.g. described in [21]) while the particle weights depend on the time variant measurements that are made in each image. Comparing Condensation with EAs it can be seen that the Condensation algorithm can be formulated as an EA with special, fixed operations: the resampling process is known as roulette-wheel parent selection, the dynamic drift of particles equals a random mutation and the replacement is always done as a generational replacement where the whole sample set is replaced by the next generation. A crossover operator that is known from Genetic Algorithms is not used in Condensation. The similarities between Condensation and EA are summarized in table 6.1. However, only few papers about adopting known principles and ideas from the research on Evolutionary Algorithms, Particle Swarms and other nature inspired heuristics to the field of visual object tracking have been published, so that the main focus in the remaining sections lies on this aspect.

Condensation	Evolutionary Algorithms
particle/sample	individual
particle/sample set	population
measurement model	fitness function
resampling	selection/replacement
dynamic drift	mutation

Table 6.1: Comparing Condensation and EAs

6.2.1 Condensation with crossover

The only operation in Condensation that updates and changes particles randomly is the application of the dynamic drift model which can be seen as a particle mutation. However, it could be beneficial to predict some of the particles using crossover techniques in order to incorporate population emergent information. The usage of a crossover operator makes it possible to exchange blocks of information between different individuals and introduces the possibility to search the state space in parallel. According to [131], mutation is able to create random diversity in the population while crossover promotes emergent behavior. Therefore, the implementation of crossover techniques might improve the performance of Condensation especially in cases where "information re-use" is important (e.g. very low number of particles).

We propose to integrate a crossover operator into the Condensation algorithm in the following way: after a particle was selected with a selection probability that is proportional to the weight (resampling step) it is either changed using crossover or using the standard dynamic drift. The percentage of the whole population that uses the crossover operator instead of the dynamic drift is determined by the crossover-rate p_c. Two different crossover operators for object tracking are implemented and evaluated in this thesis:

1. Uniform crossover: For each value $x_{t,k}$ in the state vector, a uniformly distributed random bit r_k is created to decide whether $x_{t,k}$ is copied from a second particle ($r_k = 0$) that has been chosen randomly or $x_{t,k}$ is not modified at all ($r_k = 1$).

2. Intermediate crossover: Each component $x_{t,k}$ is created using a second randomly chosen particle $\mathbf{x}'$:

$$x_{t,k} = \rho \cdot (x'_{t-1,k} - x_{t-1,k}) \tag{6.1}$$

where $\rho \in [0, 1]$ denotes a uniformly distributed random number.

The second particle that serves as a crossover partner can either be chosen from the population at time $t - 1$ or from the actual population that is newly generated. The selection from the current generation can be seen as a kind of steady-state selection (see section 2.2.1). The usage of a steady state selection could be advantageous due to the fact that the current observation is used to adapt the position of the particle. The proposed Condensation algorithm that uses recombination techniques is shown in figure 6.2.1. The different types of crossover will be evaluated in section 6.3.

```
procedure CondensationCrossover(S) : returns S
begin
    t:=0;
    initialize(S₀);
    evaluate(S₀);
    repeat
        S_{t+1}={};
        for i = 1 to N
            x_t^{(i)}=select(S_t);
            if uniform_random(0,1) < p_c then
                x'=select_random(S_t);
                x_{t+1}^{(i)}=crossover(x_t^{(i)}, x');
            else
                x_{t+1}^{(i)}=drift(x_t^{(i)});
            endif
            π_{t+1}^{(i)}=measure(x_{t+1}^{(i)});
            S_{t+1}=S_{t+1} ∪ {(x_{t+1}^{(i)}, π_{t+1}^{(i)})}
        endfor
        t:=t+1;
    until termination
end
```

Figure 6.1: Condensation with a crossover operator.

6.2.2   Condensation with swarm dynamics

In order to incorporate more knowledge from the whole population into the dynamic drift of each particle, a model inspired by the variation operator that is used in the Particle Swarm algorithm (see section 2.2.2) is proposed in the following. The main idea is to modify the dynamic model that predicts the samples and use the information that comes from the best particle. Assume that the state $\mathbf{x}_t$ of the particles consists of a velocity $\mathbf{v}_t$ and a position $\mathbf{p}_t$. Then, all particles can be attracted towards the position $\mathbf{p}^*$ of the best sample $\mathbf{x}^*$ by

$$\mathbf{v}_t = r \cdot (\mathbf{v}_{t-1} + \sigma_v \cdot \mathbf{u}_t) + (1 - r) \cdot (\mathbf{p}_t^* - \mathbf{p}_{t-1}) \tag{6.2}$$

$$\mathbf{p}_t = \mathbf{p}_{t-1} + \mathbf{v}_t \tag{6.3}$$

where $r \in [0, 1]$ denotes a uniformly distributed random number. The value of r defines how much the velocity of the particle is changed to the direction of the best particle. If $r = 1$, then $\mathbf{v}_t$ is modified using a random walk model that adds a normally distributed random vector $\mathbf{u}_t$. This is a standard dynamic drift model that is often used in Condensation. In case of $r = 0$, the velocity is set to the difference between the last position of the particle and the position of the best particle. The attraction of the position of a particle towards the best position using equation 6.2 is depicted graphically in figure 6.3 for a two-dimensional state space. In a dynamically changing search space the fitness of the best particle changes and must be updated in each time step. We propose to split the population into two parts. The first part is predicted using the best particle from the last time step and thus produces a new best particle based on the current observation. The second part of the population can then be predicted using the actual best sample that has been observed. The resampling step remains the same as in standard Condensation. The proposed algorithm that extends Condensation with swarm dynamics is depicted in figure 6.2.2.

```
procedure CondensationSwarmDynamics(S) : returns S
begin
    t:=0;
    initialize(S₀);
    evaluate(S₀);
    x₀*=update_best(S₀);
    repeat
        S_{t+1}={};
        for i = 1 to N
            x_t^{(i)}=select(S_t);
            if i < N/2 then
                x_{t+1}^{(i)}=swarm_drift(x_t^{(i)}, x_t*);
            else
                x_{t+1}^{(i)}=swarm_drift(x_t^{(i)}, x_{t+1}*);
            endif
            π_{t+1}^{(i)}=measure(x_{t+1}^{(i)});
            S_{t+1}=S_{t+1} ∪ {(x_{t+1}^{(i)}, π_{t+1}^{(i)})}
            x_{t+1}*=update_best(S_{t+1});
        endfor
        t:=t+1;
    until termination;
end
```

Figure 6.2: Condensation with swarm dynamics.

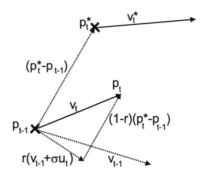

Figure 6.3: Position and velocity update using swarm dynamics.

6.3 Experiments

In this section a detailed comparison of the proposed extensions of the Condensation algorithm is performed on a set of different test sequences.

6.3.1 Dynamics and measurement models

To compare the performance of the different extensions of the Condensation algorithm, image regions are tracked that can be described by the state vector

$$\mathbf{x}_t = (x, y, s, v_x, v_y, v_s)_t^T \tag{6.4}$$

where (x, y) denotes the pixel position of the rectangular region with the scale s and (v_x, v_y, v_s) model pixel velocities in position and scale. The dynamics are modeled as a random walk:

$$\mathbf{v}_t = \mathbf{v}_{t-1} + \sigma_v \mathbf{u}_t \tag{6.5}$$
$$\mathbf{p}_t = \mathbf{p}_{t-1} + \mathbf{v}_t \tag{6.6}$$

with $\mathbf{v}_t = [v_x, v_y, v_s]_t^T$ and $\mathbf{p}_t = [x, y, s]_t^T$. This defines a movement with constant velocity and small random changes in velocity, which are incorporated by addition of a random vector $\mathbf{u}_t$.

Two different measurement models to determine the weights of the particles are used: a model based on feature classifiers that have been learned offline (see section 3.4) and a model that uses color histograms. The measurement model in case of using grayscale feature classifiers evaluates the strong classifier h at the current position of the sample.

Instead of using the output of the strong classifier, which is a binary value, the weight $\pi^{(i)}$ for each sample is set according to the weighted sum of the weak classifiers (see also [84]):

$$w = \sum_{j=1}^{T} \alpha_j h_j(x) \tag{6.7}$$

$$\pi_t^{(i)} = \frac{\exp(K \cdot (w - \theta))}{(\exp(K \cdot (w - \theta)) + \exp(K \cdot (-w + \theta)))} \tag{6.8}$$

where α_j, h_j are the weighted weak classifiers (see section 3.4) and θ is the threshold of the strong classifier. The constant parameter K specifies the slope of the likelihood function. Figure 6.4 exemplarily shows the likelihood for $K \in \{0.25, 0.5, 0.75, 1\}, \theta = 5$ and $w \in [0, 10]$. A constant value of $K = 0.5$ is used in all experiments.

To track colored objects, we use a histogram model that is similar to the work described in [107]. The weight of each particle is calculated by comparing the color distribution of the image region that is described by the particle to a reference region that has been defined offline. The color distribution is specified using a histogram in the Hue-Saturation-Value (HSV) color space [129]. Each pixel that has a saturation value above 0.1 and a hue value larger than 0.2 is counted in a histogram with $N_h \cdot N_s$ bins. Pixels that do not meet these requirements ("color-free" pixels) populate a number of N_v additional bins so that the histogram $\eta(\mathbf{x})$ for a state-vector $\mathbf{x}$ can be described as

$$\eta(\mathbf{x}) = \{\eta_1(\mathbf{x}), ..., \eta_N(\mathbf{x})\}; \quad N = N_h \cdot N_s + N_v \tag{6.9}$$

with

$$\eta_i(\mathbf{x}) = K \cdot \sum_{\mathbf{d} \in R(\mathbf{x})} \delta(b(\mathbf{d}) - i). \tag{6.10}$$

$R(\mathbf{x})$ describes the image region for the state vector $\mathbf{x}$, $b(\mathbf{d})$ maps a pixel $\mathbf{d}$ to a bin, δ is the Kronecker delta function and K denotes a normalization constant that ensures $\sum_{i=1}^{N} \eta_i(\mathbf{x}) = 1$. Given a reference histogram $\eta^*(\mathbf{z})$ of an image region $\mathbf{z}$ it is possible to calculate the distance between the histogram $\eta(\mathbf{x})$ and the reference histogram as

$$D(\eta(\mathbf{x}), \eta^*(\mathbf{z})) = \left[1 - \sum_{n=1}^{N} \sqrt{\eta_i(\mathbf{x})\eta_i^*(\mathbf{z})} \right]^{\frac{1}{2}}. \tag{6.11}$$

The weight of each particle can then be calculated as

$$p(z_t | \mathbf{x}_t) \propto exp(-\lambda D^2(\eta(\mathbf{x}_t), \eta^*(\mathbf{z}))) \tag{6.12}$$

using constant factor λ which is set to $\lambda = 20$ according to [107]. The characteristics of the likelihood for the histogram distance $D \in [0, 1]$ is shown in figure 6.4.

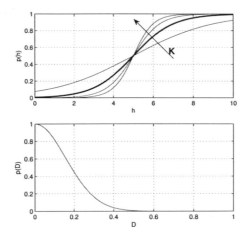

Figure 6.4: Likelihood function for grayscale features (top) and color histograms (bottom).

6.3.2   Test sequences and performance metrics

The evaluation was carried out on a set of four different test sequences that include a total number of 1960 images of the size 320x240 pixels. One sequence was created artificially and shows a colored rectangle (see figure 6.5) moving with a varying velocity in front of a background with random colored noise. The other sequences were recorded in an unconstrained office environment and show a person moving in front of a cluttered background. We recorded two colored sequences and one grayscale sequence. The movement of the person covered all three dimensions without in-plane or out-of-plane rotations. Parts of the sequences show a movement with very high velocity that causes image blurring effects (see figure 6.6) which makes the tracking even more challenging.

The ground-truth data about the real position of the object in each image was only available for the artificially created sequence. In order to get a ground-truth for the other sequences, a standard Condensation tracking algorithm that utilizes up to 10000 samples was used and the weighted mean of the state of the best samples was taken as the true position of the object. The very high number of samples guaranteed accurate position estimates but the runtime for tracking was of course far from real-time.

The algorithms were evaluated on the test sequences using the ground-truth data and the tracking metrics that are described in the following. If an object was detected in a frame and the object was visible in the ground-truth, the tracking accuracy TA was calculated as follows:

$$TA = \frac{2 \cdot n_{overlap}}{n_{detected} + n_{real}}, \tag{6.13}$$

where $n_{overlap}$ is the number of overlapping pixels between the box around the true object position and the detected position. $n_{detected}$ is the number of pixels in the box, which the tracker returns and n_{real} is the number of pixels in the rectangle around the true object position. Based on the tracking accuracy the following values can be calculated:

- Detection rate $DR = \frac{N_D}{N_P}$; N_D is the number of frames where an object was detected (with $TA \geq 0.6$) and visible in ground truth, N_P is the total number of frames where an object was visible.

- False positive rate $FPR = \frac{N_F}{N_N}$; N_F is the number of frames where an object was detected but not visible in ground truth, N_N is the total number of frames where no object was visible.

- Classification rate CR: percentage of all frames that were correctly classified ($TA \geq 0.6$ or no object in ground truth and no object detected).

As we want to evaluate the tracking algorithm itself and not the performance of the underlying measurement models the test sequences show a single moving object and they do not contain any frames where no object is visible. Therefore, the false positive rate is not defined and the classification rate CR is equal to the detection rate DR and measures the percentage of images in which the tracker did correctly lock at the object (with an accuracy above 0.6). In all experiments in this chapter the values of CR and TA are adequate for comparing the tracking performance, while FPR and DR are additionally calculated in the experiments in the next chapter (see section 7.7), where different measurement models are compared for tracking on a mobile robot.

Figure 6.5: Artificially created colored object.

Figure 6.6: Face tracking on a test sequence.

Sequence	Images	Description
Color_Sequence_1	450	Face tracking using color histogram
Color_Sequence_2	460	Face tracking using color histogram
Grey_Sequence	650	Face tracking using feature classifier
Artificial_Sequence	400	Tracking of artificial object using color histogram

Table 6.2: Test sequences.

6.3.3   Evaluation and comparison

Parameter settings

All experiments were carried out with a decreasing numbers of samples N with
$N \in \{250, 100, 50, 25, 15\}$. The sample population was initialized randomly with random positions over the whole image and normally distributed random velocities with

$\sigma_i = 4.0$. 10% of all samples were re-initialzed in each iteration in order to cope with sudden changes in object motion and the weighted sum of the best 15% of all samples was used as the estimate for the object state.

Other parameters were the standard deviation of the noise term in the dynamic model σ_v, and for Condensation with crossover one had to determine a suitable crossover rate p_c. To evaluate the parameter settings face tracking in a colored test sequence (Color_Sequence_1) was chosen and the tracking rates were calculated. Each evaluation run was repeated 20 times in order to deal with the stochastic nature of the tracking process. All depicted results are the mean tracking rates together with standard deviations.

The results for the parameter $\sigma_v \in \{1, 2, 3, 4, 6, 8\}$ for tracking with standard Condensation are shown in figure 6.4. As expected, the tracking rates decrease with a decreasing number of samples. Concerning the parameter σ_v one can see that the rates increase up to a local maximum at $\sigma_v = 3.0$ and decrease with higher values of σ_v. Of course the value of σ_v depends on the object motion in the image but since σ_v has to be fixed in standard Condensation, this value is used for all tracking experiments.

Table 6.5 shows the results of the parameter evaluation for Condensation with swarm dynamics. Here, the optimal value is $\sigma_v = 6.0$.

For tracking with the Condensation-crossover algorithm we first analyzed different crossover rates $p_c \in \{0.1, 0.2, 0.3, 0.4, 0.5, 0.6, 0.7, 0.8\}$ with a fixed value of $\sigma_v = 4.0$ due to the fact that changes in p_c should have a higher influence on the tracking results. The results (see table A.1) show that the best tracking rates can be obtained with a crossover rate between 20% and 30% so that a value of $p_c = 0.25$ is chosen for further experiments. The influence of σ_v with $p_c = 0.25$ is then depicted in table A.2 which show that the best results can be produced with a value of $\sigma_v = 6.0$. All parameters that have been set according to the experiments on the test sequence are summarized in table 6.3 and will be used in the following evaluations.

Method	Parameters
Standard Condensation	$\sigma_i = 4.0, \sigma_s = 3.0$
Swarm Dynamics Condensation	$\sigma_i = 4.0, \sigma_s = 6.0$
Crossover Condensation	$\sigma_i = 4.0, \sigma_s = 6.0, p_c = 0.25$

Table 6.3: Parameters used in the experiments.

Method	#Samples	CR mean $\pm$ std	TA mean $\pm$ std
Condensation $\sigma_v = 1.0$	250	0.98 ± 0.01	0.90 ± 0.01
Condensation $\sigma_v = 2.0$	250	0.99 ± 0.00	0.92 ± 0.00
Condensation $\sigma_v = 3.0$	250	0.99 ± 0.00	0.92 ± 0.00
Condensation $\sigma_v = 4.0$	250	0.98 ± 0.00	0.91 ± 0.00
Condensation $\sigma_v = 5.0$	250	0.97 ± 0.01	0.91 ± 0.00
Condensation $\sigma_v = 6.0$	250	0.96 ± 0.01	0.90 ± 0.00
Condensation $\sigma_v = 7.0$	250	0.94 ± 0.01	0.90 ± 0.00
Condensation $\sigma_v = 8.0$	250	0.93 ± 0.01	0.90 ± 0.00
Condensation $\sigma_v = 1.0$	100	0.89 ± 0.04	0.83 ± 0.02
Condensation $\sigma_v = 2.0$	100	0.98 ± 0.01	0.88 ± 0.01
Condensation $\sigma_v = 3.0$	100	0.97 ± 0.01	0.88 ± 0.01
Condensation $\sigma_v = 4.0$	100	0.96 ± 0.01	0.88 ± 0.00
Condensation $\sigma_v = 5.0$	100	0.95 ± 0.01	0.88 ± 0.00
Condensation $\sigma_v = 6.0$	100	0.94 ± 0.01	0.87 ± 0.00
Condensation $\sigma_v = 7.0$	100	0.92 ± 0.01	0.87 ± 0.00
Condensation $\sigma_v = 8.0$	100	0.90 ± 0.01	0.87 ± 0.00
Condensation $\sigma_v = 1.0$	50	0.72 ± 0.07	0.77 ± 0.02
Condensation $\sigma_v = 2.0$	50	0.90 ± 0.03	0.82 ± 0.01
Condensation $\sigma_v = 3.0$	50	0.91 ± 0.03	0.83 ± 0.01
Condensation $\sigma_v = 4.0$	50	0.89 ± 0.03	0.82 ± 0.01
Condensation $\sigma_v = 5.0$	50	0.90 ± 0.03	0.83 ± 0.01
Condensation $\sigma_v = 6.0$	50	0.87 ± 0.02	0.83 ± 0.01
Condensation $\sigma_v = 7.0$	50	0.85 ± 0.02	0.82 ± 0.01
Condensation $\sigma_v = 8.0$	50	0.83 ± 0.02	0.82 ± 0.00
Condensation $\sigma_v = 1.0$	25	0.41 ± 0.09	0.70 ± 0.02
Condensation $\sigma_v = 2.0$	25	0.67 ± 0.07	0.74 ± 0.02
Condensation $\sigma_v = 3.0$	25	0.72 ± 0.03	0.75 ± 0.01
Condensation $\sigma_v = 4.0$	25	0.70 ± 0.04	0.75 ± 0.01
Condensation $\sigma_v = 5.0$	25	0.68 ± 0.05	0.76 ± 0.01
Condensation $\sigma_v = 6.0$	25	0.69 ± 0.03	0.76 ± 0.01
Condensation $\sigma_v = 7.0$	25	0.66 ± 0.03	0.76 ± 0.01
Condensation $\sigma_v = 8.0$	25	0.62 ± 0.03	0.76 ± 0.01
Condensation $\sigma_v = 1.0$	15	0.21 ± 0.06	0.66 ± 0.03
Condensation $\sigma_v = 2.0$	15	0.39 ± 0.08	0.69 ± 0.02
Condensation $\sigma_v = 3.0$	15	0.45 ± 0.05	0.71 ± 0.01
Condensation $\sigma_v = 4.0$	15	0.45 ± 0.04	0.71 ± 0.02
Condensation $\sigma_v = 5.0$	15	0.42 ± 0.05	0.71 ± 0.01
Condensation $\sigma_v = 6.0$	15	0.41 ± 0.04	0.71 ± 0.01
Condensation $\sigma_v = 7.0$	15	0.39 ± 0.04	0.71 ± 0.01
Condensation $\sigma_v = 8.0$	15	0.35 ± 0.03	0.71 ± 0.01

Table 6.4: Tracking performance for standard Condensation with different parameter σ_v

Method	#Samples	CR mean ± std	TA mean ± std
CondensationSwarm $\sigma_v = 1.0$	250	0.95 ± 0.04	0.86 ± 0.03
CondensationSwarm $\sigma_v = 2.0$	250	0.96 ± 0.04	0.88 ± 0.03
CondensationSwarm $\sigma_v = 3.0$	250	0.98 ± 0.03	0.90 ± 0.02
CondensationSwarm $\sigma_v = 4.0$	250	0.96 ± 0.04	0.89 ± 0.02
CondensationSwarm $\sigma_v = 5.0$	250	0.96 ± 0.02	0.89 ± 0.02
CondensationSwarm $\sigma_v = 6.0$	250	0.95 ± 0.05	0.89 ± 0.03
CondensationSwarm $\sigma_v = 7.0$	250	0.96 ± 0.04	0.89 ± 0.03
CondensationSwarm $\sigma_v = 8.0$	250	0.96 ± 0.04	0.89 ± 0.03
CondensationSwarm $\sigma_v = 1.0$	100	0.90 ± 0.06	0.83 ± 0.04
CondensationSwarm $\sigma_v = 2.0$	100	0.93 ± 0.05	0.85 ± 0.03
CondensationSwarm $\sigma_v = 3.0$	100	0.97 ± 0.03	0.89 ± 0.02
CondensationSwarm $\sigma_v = 4.0$	100	0.97 ± 0.04	0.89 ± 0.02
CondensationSwarm $\sigma_v = 5.0$	100	0.96 ± 0.05	0.89 ± 0.03
CondensationSwarm $\sigma_v = 6.0$	100	0.96 ± 0.04	0.88 ± 0.03
CondensationSwarm $\sigma_v = 7.0$	100	0.95 ± 0.04	0.89 ± 0.03
CondensationSwarm $\sigma_v = 8.0$	100	0.95 ± 0.04	0.89 ± 0.03
CondensationSwarm $\sigma_v = 1.0$	50	0.86 ± 0.06	0.80 ± 0.03
CondensationSwarm $\sigma_v = 2.0$	50	0.93 ± 0.05	0.84 ± 0.02
CondensationSwarm $\sigma_v = 3.0$	50	0.93 ± 0.06	0.85 ± 0.03
CondensationSwarm $\sigma_v = 4.0$	50	0.94 ± 0.04	0.86 ± 0.02
CondensationSwarm $\sigma_v = 5.0$	50	0.94 ± 0.05	0.86 ± 0.03
CondensationSwarm $\sigma_v = 6.0$	50	0.95 ± 0.05	0.87 ± 0.03
CondensationSwarm $\sigma_v = 7.0$	50	0.96 ± 0.04	0.88 ± 0.02
CondensationSwarm $\sigma_v = 8.0$	50	0.96 ± 0.04	0.88 ± 0.02
CondensationSwarm $\sigma_v = 1.0$	25	0.70 ± 0.08	0.75 ± 0.04
CondensationSwarm $\sigma_v = 2.0$	25	0.83 ± 0.06	0.79 ± 0.03
CondensationSwarm $\sigma_v = 3.0$	25	0.88 ± 0.06	0.81 ± 0.04
CondensationSwarm $\sigma_v = 4.0$	25	0.90 ± 0.06	0.82 ± 0.03
CondensationSwarm $\sigma_v = 5.0$	25	0.92 ± 0.04	0.83 ± 0.03
CondensationSwarm $\sigma_v = 6.0$	25	0.94 ± 0.04	0.84 ± 0.02
CondensationSwarm $\sigma_v = 7.0$	25	0.93 ± 0.04	0.84 ± 0.02
CondensationSwarm $\sigma_v = 8.0$	25	0.93 ± 0.04	0.84 ± 0.02
CondensationSwarm $\sigma_v = 1.0$	15	0.51 ± 0.07	0.74 ± 0.03
CondensationSwarm $\sigma_v = 2.0$	15	0.67 ± 0.07	0.75 ± 0.02
CondensationSwarm $\sigma_v = 3.0$	15	0.76 ± 0.06	0.76 ± 0.03
CondensationSwarm $\sigma_v = 4.0$	15	0.82 ± 0.04	0.78 ± 0.02
CondensationSwarm $\sigma_v = 5.0$	15	0.86 ± 0.05	0.80 ± 0.02
CondensationSwarm $\sigma_v = 6.0$	15	0.87 ± 0.05	0.80 ± 0.03
CondensationSwarm $\sigma_v = 7.0$	15	0.88 ± 0.05	0.80 ± 0.02
CondensationSwarm $\sigma_v = 8.0$	15	0.88 ± 0.05	0.80 ± 0.02

Table 6.5: Tracking performance for Condensation with swarm dynamics with different parameter σ_v.

Evaluation and comparison

In a first experiment, four different crossover techniques were compared: uniform, intermediate, uniform with steady-state selection and intermediate with steady-state selection. The steady-state selection scheme selects the crossover partner from the actual population at time t while the selection in the other case is performed randomly over all samples from the last population $t - 1$. The results of the comparison on Color_Sequence_1 are shown in figure 6.7 and table 6.6. The intermediate crossover always outperformed the uniform crossover. The advantage of the intermediate technique is that the state of the sample that is created can have continuous values between the two states of the crossover partners while a uniform crossover is always discrete and does not introduce many different new states. The experiments also approved the assumption that a steady-state selection should be preferred because the current population at time t and therefore measurements on the actual image are used to update the sample states. Thus, for all experiments in this section intermediate crossover with steady state selection is used.

In case of using swarm dynamics, we proposed to update the second half of the whole population using the best particle from the current population. This technique was compared to an update of all particles using always the best samples from the last position. The results of the comparison on Color_Sequence_1 can be found in figure 6.8 and table 6.7. There were no significant differences in the tracking rate CR but an update towards the current best position resulted in slightly higher values for the tracking accuracy TA so that this technique will be used in all following experiments.

In the following, the tracking performance of standard Condensation, Condensation with crossover and Condensation with swarm dynamics was compared on the different test sequences. The results on the artificially created sequence showed a clear advantage of the Swarm-Condensation compared to the other techniques (see figure 6.9 and table 6.8). The tracking rates of the other methods dropped below 50% using less than 100 particles while Swarm-Condensation was able to achieve a rate of $CR = 93\%$ using only 15 samples. Here, the difference between standard condensation and the crossover technique was only small. The tracking rates on the two colored sequences show more or less the same trend (see figures 6.10 and 6.11 and tables 6.9 and 6.10). If the number of samples dropped below $N = 100$ the newly proposed algorithms outperformed standard Condensation while Swarm-Condensation achieved the best tracking results. Combining Condensation with crossover yielded the best results compared to the other techniques when a higher number of samples (more than 50) was used. Finally, figure 6.12 and table 6.11 depict the results of the comparison on the tracking in the gray-sequence using feature classifiers. Due to the fact that in this sequence many local optima of the measurement function exist that could detract the tracker the rates CR were generally lower for a low number of samples compared to the previous experiments. Stable tracking with only 15 samples was not possible in this sequence, however, Swarm-Condensation was able to achieve a mean tracking rate of $CR = 74\%$ using only 25 samples while the rates of the other techniques dropped below 50%.

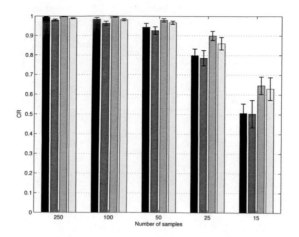

Figure 6.7: Comparison of the classification rate CR with different crossover techniques (from left to right: uniform+steady-state, uniform, intermediate+steady-state, intermediate).

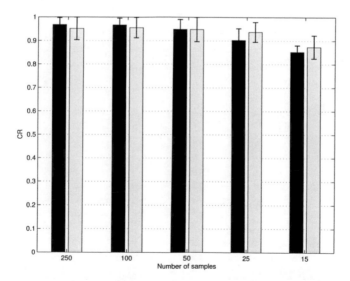

Figure 6.8: Comparison of the classification rate CR with different swarm dynamics (left: use last-best particle, right: use actual-best particle).

Method	#Samples	CR mean ± std	TA mean ± std
Crossover uniform, steady-State	250	0.99 ± 0.00	0.92 ± 0.00
Crossover uniform	250	0.98 ± 0.01	0.91 ± 0.00
Crossover intermediate, steady-state	250	1.00 ± 0.00	0.93 ± 0.00
Crossover intermediate	250	0.99 ± 0.00	0.92 ± 0.00
Crossover uniform, steady-State	100	0.98 ± 0.01	0.89 ± 0.00
Crossover uniform	100	0.96 ± 0.01	0.89 ± 0.00
Crossover intermediate, steady-state	100	1.00 ± 0.00	0.90 ± 0.00
Crossover intermediate	100	0.98 ± 0.01	0.90 ± 0.00
Crossover uniform, steady-State	50	0.94 ± 0.02	0.85 ± 0.01
Crossover uniform	50	0.93 ± 0.02	0.84 ± 0.01
Crossover intermediate, steady-state	50	0.98 ± 0.01	0.87 ± 0.01
Crossover intermediate	50	0.97 ± 0.01	0.86 ± 0.00
Crossover uniform, steady-State	25	0.80 ± 0.03	0.78 ± 0.01
Crossover uniform	25	0.79 ± 0.04	0.78 ± 0.01
Crossover intermediate, steady-state	25	0.90 ± 0.02	0.81 ± 0.01
Crossover intermediate	25	0.86 ± 0.03	0.80 ± 0.01
Crossover uniform, steady-State	15	0.51 ± 0.05	0.72 ± 0.02
Crossover uniform	15	0.50 ± 0.07	0.72 ± 0.01
Crossover intermediate, steady-state	15	0.65 ± 0.04	0.74 ± 0.01
Crossover intermediate	15	0.63 ± 0.06	0.74 ± 0.01

Table 6.6: Tracking performance of different crossover techniques.

Method	#Samples	CR mean ± std	TA mean ± std
CondensationSwarm, last-best	250	0.97 ± 0.03	0.88 ± 0.02
CondensationSwarm, actual-best	250	0.95 ± 0.05	0.89 ± 0.03
CondensationSwarm, last-best	100	0.97 ± 0.03	0.86 ± 0.02
CondensationSwarm, actual-best	100	0.96 ± 0.04	0.88 ± 0.03
CondensationSwarm, last-best	50	0.95 ± 0.04	0.85 ± 0.02
CondensationSwarm, actual-best	50	0.95 ± 0.05	0.87 ± 0.03
CondensationSwarm, last-best	25	0.90 ± 0.05	0.81 ± 0.03
CondensationSwarm, actual-best	25	0.94 ± 0.04	0.84 ± 0.02
CondensationSwarm, last-best	15	0.85 ± 0.03	0.77 ± 0.02
CondensationSwarm, actual-best	15	0.87 ± 0.05	0.80 ± 0.03

Table 6.7: Tracking performance of different swarm dynamics.

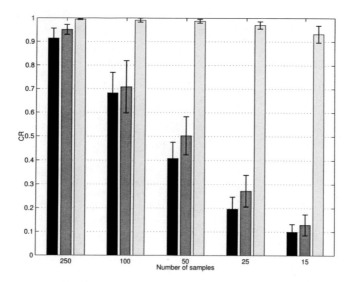

Figure 6.9: Comparison of the classification rate CR on artificial-sequence (from left to right: Condensation, CondensationCrossover, CondensationSwarm).

Method	#Samples	CR mean ± std	TA mean ± std
Condensation	250	0.91 ± 0.04	0.88 ± 0.01
CondensationCrossover	250	0.95 ± 0.02	0.88 ± 0.00
CondensationSwarm	250	0.99 ± 0.00	0.92 ± 0.00
Condensation	100	0.68 ± 0.09	0.84 ± 0.01
CondensationCrossover	100	0.71 ± 0.11	0.85 ± 0.01
CondensationSwarm	100	0.99 ± 0.01	0.91 ± 0.00
Condensation	50	0.41 ± 0.07	0.79 ± 0.02
CondensationCrossover	50	0.50 ± 0.08	0.81 ± 0.01
CondensationSwarm	50	0.99 ± 0.01	0.90 ± 0.00
Condensation	25	0.20 ± 0.05	0.72 ± 0.03
CondensationCrossover	25	0.27 ± 0.07	0.76 ± 0.02
CondensationSwarm	25	0.97 ± 0.02	0.88 ± 0.01
Condensation	15	0.10 ± 0.03	0.68 ± 0.03
CondensationCrossover	15	0.13 ± 0.04	0.71 ± 0.04
CondensationSwarm	15	0.93 ± 0.04	0.84 ± 0.01

Table 6.8: Tracking performance on artificial-sequence.

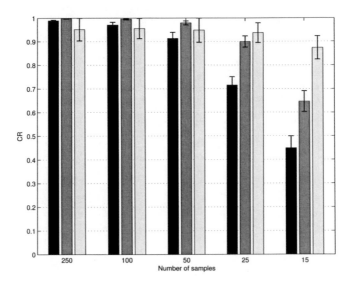

Figure 6.10: Comparison of the classification rate CR on color-sequence_1 (from left to right: Condensation, CondensationCrossover, CondensationSwarm).

Method	#Samples	CR mean $\pm$ std	TA mean $\pm$ std
Condensation	250	0.99 ± 0.00	0.92 ± 0.00
CondensationCrossover	250	1.00 ± 0.00	0.93 ± 0.00
CondensationSwarm	250	0.95 ± 0.05	0.89 ± 0.03
Condensation	100	0.97 ± 0.01	0.88 ± 0.01
CondensationCrossover	100	1.00 ± 0.00	0.90 ± 0.00
CondensationSwarm	100	0.96 ± 0.04	0.88 ± 0.03
Condensation	50	0.91 ± 0.03	0.83 ± 0.01
CondensationCrossover	50	0.98 ± 0.01	0.87 ± 0.01
CondensationSwarm	50	0.95 ± 0.05	0.87 ± 0.03
Condensation	25	0.72 ± 0.03	0.75 ± 0.01
CondensationCrossover	25	0.90 ± 0.02	0.81 ± 0.01
CondensationSwarm	25	0.94 ± 0.04	0.84 ± 0.02
Condensation	15	0.45 ± 0.05	0.71 ± 0.01
CondensationCrossover	15	0.65 ± 0.04	0.74 ± 0.01
CondensationSwarm	15	0.87 ± 0.05	0.80 ± 0.03

Table 6.9: Tracking performance for color-sequence_1.

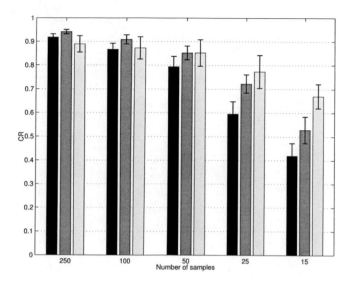

Figure 6.11: Comparison of the classification rate CR on color-sequence_2 (from left to right: Condensation, CondensationCrossover, CondensationSwarm).

Method	#Samples	CR mean $\pm$ std	TA mean $\pm$ std
Condensation	250	0.92 ± 0.01	0.74 ± 0.00
CondensationCrossover	250	0.94 ± 0.01	0.75 ± 0.00
CondensationSwarm	250	0.89 ± 0.04	0.74 ± 0.02
Condensation	100	0.87 ± 0.03	0.72 ± 0.01
CondensationCrossover	100	0.91 ± 0.02	0.74 ± 0.00
CondensationSwarm	100	0.87 ± 0.05	0.73 ± 0.03
Condensation	50	0.79 ± 0.04	0.70 ± 0.01
CondensationCrossover	50	0.85 ± 0.03	0.72 ± 0.01
CondensationSwarm	50	0.85 ± 0.06	0.72 ± 0.04
Condensation	25	0.60 ± 0.05	0.62 ± 0.02
CondensationCrossover	25	0.72 ± 0.04	0.67 ± 0.02
CondensationSwarm	25	0.77 ± 0.07	0.68 ± 0.04
Condensation	15	0.42 ± 0.05	0.53 ± 0.03
CondensationCrossover	15	0.53 ± 0.06	0.58 ± 0.03
CondensationSwarm	15	0.67 ± 0.05	0.64 ± 0.02

Table 6.10: Tracking performance on color-sequence_2.

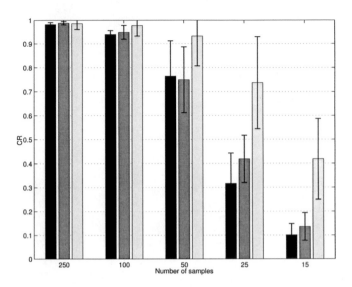

Figure 6.12: Comparison of the classification rate CR on gray-sequence (from left to right: Condensation, CondensationCrossover, CondensationSwarm).

Method	#Samples	CR mean $\pm$ std	TA mean $\pm$ std
Condensation	250	0.98 ± 0.01	0.84 ± 0.00
CondensationCrossover	250	0.99 ± 0.01	0.84 ± 0.00
CondensationSwarm	250	0.99 ± 0.02	0.89 ± 0.02
Condensation	100	0.94 ± 0.02	0.81 ± 0.01
CondensationCrossover	100	0.95 ± 0.03	0.81 ± 0.02
CondensationSwarm	100	0.98 ± 0.04	0.87 ± 0.03
Condensation	50	0.76 ± 0.15	0.71 ± 0.09
CondensationCrossover	50	0.75 ± 0.14	0.69 ± 0.10
CondensationSwarm	50	0.93 ± 0.13	0.84 ± 0.10
Condensation	25	0.32 ± 0.13	0.46 ± 0.13
CondensationCrossover	25	0.42 ± 0.10	0.51 ± 0.09
CondensationSwarm	25	0.74 ± 0.19	0.70 ± 0.14
Condensation	15	0.10 ± 0.05	0.28 ± 0.10
CondensationCrossover	15	0.14 ± 0.06	0.30 ± 0.09
CondensationSwarm	15	0.42 ± 0.17	0.49 ± 0.16

Table 6.11: Tracking performance on gray-sequence.

6.4   Related work

Outside the area of computer vision, Higuchi proposed a Monte Carlo filter with Genetic Algorithm operations [63]. Higuchi encoded each component of the state vector as a bit string to be able to apply mutation (random bit flip) and crossover (1-point). A crossover and mutation rate was defined independently for each vector component. The dynamical model without random noise (growth model) which was not seen as a mutation was applied before using the genetic operators. The algorithm was tested on a simple artificial time-series problem and the problem of estimating trends in seasonal adjustment.

Tito et al. [137] proposed a Genetic Particle Filter, where crossover and mutation operators were executed before the application of the dynamic model. Additionally, the authors suggested the usage of the so called Metropolis algorithm criterion for the replacement of the parent population: newly created particles were accepted, if their weights were larger than the weights of the parents, otherwise acceptance occurred only with a certain probability. The disadvantage of using this criterion is that the weights of parents have to be recalculated in each time step on the actual input data to be comparable with the weights of their children, which leads to higher computational time. The algorithm was evaluated on an artificial simulation of non-linear time series.

For the problem of body motion tracking in the context of motion capturing, Deutscher et al. [38] used an Annealed Particle Filter in combination with a 2-point-crossover. The authors showed that the runtime for processing one frame could be reduced from 60 seconds to 15 seconds (Pentium III 1GHz) by the application of their extended method.

Cui and Sun [35] proposed a so called GA-based Particle Filter to track 3D hand motions in images. In this framework, a Genetic Algorithm was used to optimize particles in each tracking step. All particles that were updated with the Particle Filter were used as an initial population for the GA which optimized the solutions over a number of additional iterations. To keep the same computational complexity as a standard Particle Filter the number of particles that were used had to be 10 times less. Keeping the same time complexity in this way, the authors showed improved tracking performance on synthetic and real test data.

The only known work until now that utilizes a hybridization of Particle Filters and Particle Swarms was published by Krohling in [78]. This approach differs from the method that was proposed in this thesis by the fact that the update of all particles toward the best particle was not integrated in the motion model but replaced the resampling step. Particles were attracted towards the best particle from the last time step and no fitness proportional resampling was carried out. Another difference is that the best particle was not updated on the current observation and thus did not improve the tracking performance by adding additional information about the current observation. The algorithm was tested on a simulated one dimensional state estimation problem (estimation of a nonlinear time-variant function) where the author was not able to show a significant improvement over a standard Particle Filter.

6.5   Summary

In this chapter the problem of reducing the number of samples while maintaining a good tracking accuracy of the Condensation algorithm was addressed. The similarities between heuristic optimization in dynamic environments and the Condensation algorithm made it possible to propose two different extensions of the Condensation algorithm, using a crossover operator and swarm dynamics. The crossover replaces the dynamic drift of a particle and changes the state, using information from a second sample, while the swarm dynamics changes the drift of each particle towards the actually best position. Both extensions were developed in order to reuse information that is already contained in the population of samples so that the population size can be decreased.

The algorithms were evaluated on a set of test sequences for face tracking in an unconstrained environment, using color histograms and grayscale feature classifiers. Different crossover operators that use uniform and intermediate crossover with and without steady state selection were implemented and a comparison between the crossover techniques revealed that the best tracking result can be achieved using the steady state intermediate operator. In all experiments both methods outperformed the standard Condensation algorithm on all test sequences when the number of samples is reduced. The best results were achieved with the Condensation algorithm that uses swarm dynamics.

Chapter 7

Application: People Identification on Mobile Robots

7.1 Introduction

In this chapter a complete system to detect, track and recognize people on a mobile robot is described. The main focus lies on the description of a new method to track people using data from a thermal camera which is one of the first approaches that has been proposed to run on a mobile robot using infrared information. A thermal camera is more suitable for tracking people than a standard color camera because a person has a very distinctive profile in thermal images and the detection is independent from current light conditions. In order to achieve fast and robust tracking, a new measurement model based on an elliptical contour model of the upper body part of a person is introduced. This model is compared to a feature based model that has been learned on thermal data. Tracking in the thermal image is used to get a first estimate of the person such that the robot is able to approach the person. When the robot is close to a person, a combination of a feature based classifier and a Condensation tracking algorithm that was introduced in chapter 6 is used here to track the face of a person in grayscale images. The image regions from the face tracker are evaluated using a face recognition algorithm that updates the probability for a person's identity over time. The work that is described in this chapter was published in [140, 141] and [31].

7.2 Tracking and recognizing people on mobile robots

The ability to interact with people in populated environments is important for mobile robots that fulfill tasks in cooperation with humans (e.g., service robots, inspection tasks, surveillance). Most of the systems to track and detect people on a mobile robot use either range sensors, like laserscanners [44, 124, 97], or a color camera as a primary sensor [119, 42, 43, 95, 12, 22, 169]. Color vision and range sensor information have also been combined to fulfill the tracking task [79, 18, 159].

The approaches that are solely based on laser scans usually try to detect the legs of a person. However, leg detection in a two-dimensional scan at a fixed height does not provide very rich and robust features to discriminate between people and other moving objects in the environment so that false positive classifications can occur. A visual sensor provides richer information and methods for people detection in color images that extract visual features like e.g. skin color, motion and depth information have been used on a mobile robot: Feyrer and Zell [42, 43] combine skin color, shape, motion and depth information to track a single person that faces the robot. Schlegel et al. [119] extract a color histogram from the shirt of person and combine color blob tracking with a contour-based approach. Tracking of the head-shoulder contour and the hand silhouette is used in [95] to build a human-robot interface. Color histograms, optical flow and an extension of the background substraction technique is used by Zajdel et al.[169] who developed a system that keeps track of humans who leave the field of view of the robot and re-enter. Wilhelm et al. [159] track skin-colored regions in the image and combine this information with sonar data to get an estimate of the position of a person that is close to the robot. Barreto et al. [12] describe a human-robot interface that relies purely on a face detector in combination with face recognition based on principal component analysis (PCA). Similar work can be found in Brèthes et al. [22], where a detected face region is tracked with color information. Both approaches additionally detect the hand in order to enable an interaction based on gestures. Blanco et al. [18] integrate face detection and laser range data and Lang et al. [79] combine several cues including sonar, laser scanner, sound localization and color image processing.

Many of the approaches assume that people are close to the robot and face toward it so that methods based on skin color and face detection can be applied. All methods for detecting and tracking people in color images on a moving platform face the problems that arise from the sensor modalities so that the performance of the systems heavily depends on the light conditions, the viewing angle, the distance and the variability of appearance of different people in the image. Thermal vision helps to overcome some of the problems related to color vision sensors, since humans have a distinctive thermal profile compared to non-living objects, and there are no large differences in the appearance between different persons in the thermal image. Another advantage using thermal images is that the sensor data does not depend on different light conditions and people can also be detected in complete darkness.

The work presented here was part of a robotic security guard project, where one task for the mobile robot is to identify people in the building while patrolling. In this scenario the robot must be able to detect a person even from larger distances, and it cannot be assumed that the person faces the direction of the robot. Therefore, skin color cannot be used as a cue for the position of a person in the image. This problem is addressed by the introduction of a new method to detect and track a person in thermal images. This information is used to get a first estimate of the position of a person relative to the robot. While tracking a person in the thermal image, the robot tries to get closer to identify the person. Identification is performed using gray value images.

7.3 System Overview

The proposed approach to identify people in real time on a mobile robot is shown in figure 7.1. The system can be divided into 4 parts. First of all, the robot starts in the search mode where it tries to detect a person based on the information from the thermal camera. If a person is detected in the thermal image the robot drives toward the person while tracking. This part is the attention system where the robot tries to get a rough estimate of the person's position based on thermal images. If the robot is close to a person we use gray value images from the pan tilt camera to track the face. While tracking the face, images from the face tracker are fed into the recognition system to update an estimate of the identity of the person. The robotic platform for the implementation of the approach in

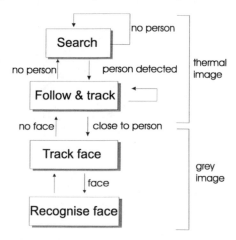

Figure 7.1: Overview over the proposed system.

this chapter is an ActiveMedia PeopleBot (see figure 7.2) which is especially designed for robot human interaction. The robot is based on a differential drive Pioneer robot platform [1] which is equipped with 24 sonar range sensors and a SICK laser scanner [4]. On top of this base, approximately at a persons shoulder-height, there is a pan tilt color camera, a thermal camera (NEC Thermo Trace [3] and a panoramic vision device mounted. For the image processing experiments in this thesis, only information from the pan tilt and thermal camera is used. The thermal camera belongs to the class of passive infrared systems which capture the thermal energy that is emitted from warm objects and convert it into a gray value image where the value of each pixel specifies the temperature (high temperatures are related to high pixel values). In contrast to this, active infrared systems use infrared light bulbs to light the scene and record the reflected light with a standard CCD camera. Active infrared systems are therefore less suitable to detect warm objects like human bodies. The specifications of the thermal camera that has been used for the experiments in this thesis are depicted in table 7.1.

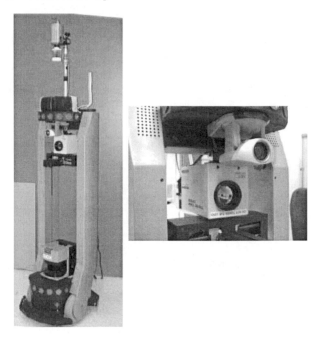

Figure 7.2: ActivMedia Peoplebot (left), thermal and pan tilt camera unit (right).

Temperature range	Range 1: -40°C-120°C
	Range 2: 0°C-500°C
	Range 3: 200°C-2000°C
Temperature resolution	0.08°C
Image resolution	320x240
Field of view	29° horizontal and 22° vertical
Focusing range	50cm to infinity
Frame rate	1/7.5 sec, 1/30 sec, 1/60 sec
Video output	NTSC/PAL video signal, S-video signal
Power consumption	approx. 5W
Weight	approx 1.4 kg

Table 7.1: Specifications for NEC Thermo Tracer TS7302 (from [3])

7.4   Tracking People in Thermal Images

The advantage of using sensor information from a thermal camera is that a person in the thermal image has a very distinctive profile so that the person can be clearly separated from the background. In figure 7.3 one can see that in the color image there is hardly any skin color visible if the person is further away, even though the person faces toward the camera. On the other hand one can easily detect the person in the same scene shown by the thermal image. However, apart from the work published in [30], where Cielniak and Duckett use image segmentation based on thresholding, noise filtering and morphological operations, there is hardly any published work on using thermal sensor information to detect humans on mobile robots until now. Infrared sensors have been applied to detect pedestrians in a driving assistance system: Bertozzi at al. [16] use a template based approach while Nanda and Davis [100] apply different image filtering techniques. Meis et al. [94] also filter the whole image and classify based on the symmetry calculated for gradients. Xu et al. [166] employ a classification method based on a support vector machine. However, template based detection as well as SVM classification and image filtering over the whole image is time consuming. Xu et al. reported a frame-rate of their system of about 5Hz and the frame rate of the system proposed in [100] lies between 3Hz and 11Hz, depending on the image resolution.

Figure 7.3: Person in color (left) and thermal image (right).

7.4.1   Tracking with Elliptic Contour Model

To track a person in the thermal image a Particle Filter and a simple elliptic model, which is very fast to calculate, is used. For each sample an elliptic contour measurement model is calculated to estimate the position of a person in the image: one ellipse describes the position of the body part and one ellipse measures the position of the head part. Therefore, one ends up with a 9-dimensional state vector: $\mathbf{x}_t = (x, y, w, h, d, v_x, v_y, v_w, v_h)$ where (x, y) is the mid-point of the body ellipse with a certain width w and height h. The height of the head is calculated by dividing h by a constant factor. The displacement of the middle of the head part from the middle of the body ellipse is described by d. The model velocities of the body part are modelled as (v_x, v_y, v_w, v_h). The elliptic contour model can be seen in figure 7.4. In this work, an upper body model is favored over a full body model, because the legs of a person are not visible in the thermal image if the person is close to the robot.

To calculate the weight $\pi_t^{(i)}$ of a sample i with state $\mathbf{x}_t^{(i)}$ the ellipses are divided into different regions (see figure 7.5) and for each region j the image gradient Δ_j between pixels in the inner part and pixels in the outer part of the ellipse is calculated. The gradient is maximal if the ellipses fit to the contour of a person in the image data. A fitness value $f^{(i)}$ for each sample i is then calculated as the sum of all gradients multiplied with a penalty factor W to reduce the total fitness in the case that a low or negative gradient exists in a certain region:

$$f^{(i)} = W \cdot \sum_{j=1}^{m} \Delta_j \tag{7.1}$$

with

$$W = \sum_{j=1}^{m} w_j, \quad w_j = \left\{ \begin{array}{ccl} 0 & : & \text{if } \Delta_j < \tau \\ \alpha_j & : & \text{otherwise} \end{array} \right. \tag{7.2}$$

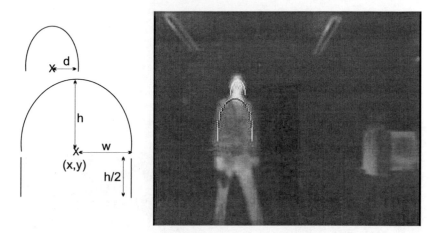

Figure 7.4: The elliptic measurement model in thermal images.

The value τ defines a gradient threshold and the weights α_j sum up to one and are chosen in a way that the shoulder parts have lower weight to minimize the measurement error that occurs due to different arm positions (see figure 7.6). The weight of each sample is calculated as the normalized fitness over all samples and the tracker claims a detection if the weighted mean of the fitness of the 20% of the best samples lies above a threshold.

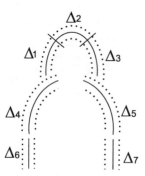

Figure 7.5: Elliptic model divided into 7 sections.

The dynamic model that is used for the Particle Filter is a simple random walk: a movement with constant velocity plus small random changes is modelled. The approach to track the contour of a person in the image is similar to the work by Isard and Blake [66] for tracking people in gray images. However, they use a spline model of the head and shoulder contour, which cannot be applied in our case, because in situations, where the person is far away or visible in a side view, there is no recognizable head-shoulder contour. The elliptic contour model is able to cope with these situations. The second advantage of using our contour model is that it can be calculated very quickly due to the fact that we measure only differences between pixel values on the inner and outer part of the ellipse.

In figure 7.7 one can see the results of tracking a person under different views at different distances. Starting with a frontal view the person turns to a side view, back view and again to a frontal position at the end.

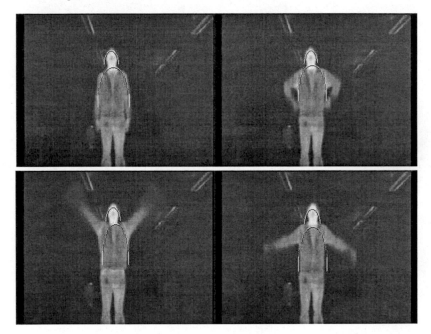

Figure 7.6: Tracking with different arm positions.

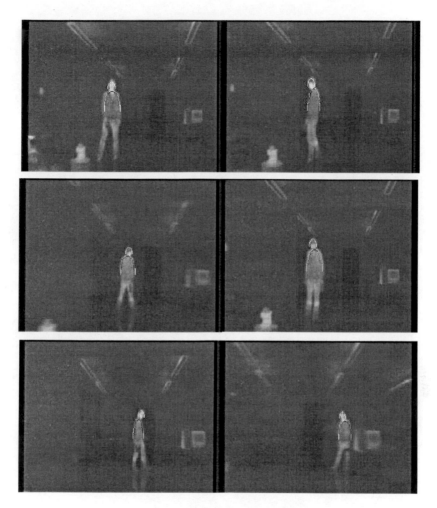

Figure 7.7: Tracking under different views.

7.4.2 Tracking with Feature Model

To build an alternative measurement model based on gray value features, the Adaboost algorithm that has been introduced in chapter 3 is used. A single strong classifier is trained, and instead of scanning the classifier over the whole image at every location and every scale, to detect a person, Particle Filtering is used again. Each sample describes a possible person located at position (x, y) and having the width w. Therefore, the state vector becomes $x_t = (x, y, w)$. The height h can be calculated by multiplying w with a constant factor, depending on the size of the training images. To calculate the weight $\pi_t^{(i)}$, the classifier is evaluated at the particle's position. Instead of using the binary output of the classifier, we rate each sample according to the weighted sum of all T features that are part of the strong classifier: $\pi_t^{(i)} = \delta \sum_{j=1}^{T} \alpha_j h_j(x_t)$, where α_j, h_j are the weighted weak classifiers (see section 3.4). To train the feature based model, a database with 106 images (positive examples) is collected, showing the upper body part of different people under different views, and 5784 images that do not show a person (negative examples) in the thermal image. The images have the size of 20x32 pixels and are normalized to have zero mean and an equal variance. Figure 7.8 shows some of the images from the training set. The model is trained until the whole database was classified correctly, which results in a strong classifier with one cascade level consisting of 29 different features.

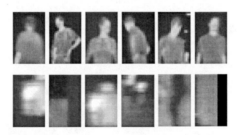

Figure 7.8: Thermal images from the person training set: person (top row) and none-person (bottom row) images.

7.4.3 Combining Contour and Feature Model

To combine the two models a cascaded model evaluation is proposed: For each sample, the feature model is evaluated first, because this evaluation is less time consuming than the calculation of the contour. If the evaluation of the feature model returns a negative classification, the weight of the particle is set to zero. In the case of a positive classification, the weight of the particle is set to the result of the contour evaluation.

7.5 Face Tracking and Recognition

A method for tracking faces using Condensation and a gray feature model that is trained with the Adaboost algorithm has been implemented on the robot and is used to focus attention on the face part if the person is close to the robot. The face tracker is trained to detect faces under slightly different views, and the detected region can also contain parts of the background. As the face recognition approach is sensitive to different positions of the face center within the located face region, we scan this region to crop out a close area that contains only facial features (see figure 7.9).

Figure 7.9: Face detection (black box: tracked face region, white box: cropped region for face recognition).

To identify the person we use a face recognition algorithm based on the well-known Eigenface approach [147]. Face regions that are extracted by the face tracker are used to update the probability of the person's identity. Therefore, each face region is rescaled, normalized and projected onto the face-space. The Euclidean distances to each face from the database in the face space is used to calculate the probabilities for each identity. Instead of recognizing each frame independently from the next frame (still-to-still recognition) we use each frame to update the identity probability with a Bayesian update rule. If the probability exceeds a certain threshold, the robot announces the estimated identity using its speech synthesizer. Figure 7.10 shows the face recognition process.

7.6 Robot Controller

The robot controller was implemented with the framework Aria (Advanced Robotics Interface for Applications) [2] that is provided by ActiveMedia. The object oriented library allows the implementation of a behavior based robot control using different actions that

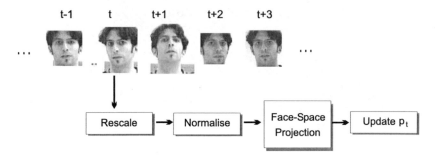

Figure 7.10: Face recognition.

are implemented by the user. The actions are resolved with user-specified priorities while being executed on the robot. The robot controller that enables a person following behavior was implemented in an action *ArActionPersonFollow*. Within this action there exist three different internal states:

- Search: this state is the initial and fall-back state, where the robot does not move and rotates stepwise. The rotation is not continuous because turning produces unwanted image blurring in the thermal image which introduces error in the detection.

- Follow: the robot detected a person in the thermal image and tracking in the thermal image is active. The translational velocity of the robot is set to a predefined value and the heading is controlled using a simple reactive controller that reacts on the relative lateral position of the person in the thermal image to adjust the heading of the robot such that the position of the person in the image is kept central. Short periods where the person is leaving the robot's field of view do not interrupt the follow behavior.

- Track face: in this state the velocity of the robot is set to zero and the pan-tilt unit is controlled using the information about the position of the face that is calculated by the face-tracker. The behavior is started when the person has a certain size in the thermal image which implies that the robot is close to the person.

The internal states are switched according to the flow chart in figure 7.1. A second action *ArActionAvoidFront*, which has a higher priority, was used to provide a simple obstacle avoidance behavior that relies on the robot's infrared sensors: if an obstacle is detected by the sensors, the robot turns in the direction, where the sensors indicate a free way.

Method	TA	CR	DR	FPR	*time*
Contour	80.2	89.8	87.7	7.4	11ms
Gray features	90.2	93.3	98.4	12.7	11ms
Combination	92.9	92.7	90.8	4.8	14ms

Table 7.2: Tracking results on test sequences.

7.7 Experiments

To test the performance of the approach we recorded test sequences with 17 different persons. In each sequence a person stood 4 to 5 meters from the robot in an unconstrained indoor environment, and the robot was started facing away from the person so that it had to turn around and search for the person in the thermal image. While tracking the person in the thermal image, the robot approached and used its pan-tilt camera to extract the face region using the method described in section 7.5. After the face had been detected, the person walked to a different position behind the robot and the robot approached a second time, so that we recorded each person under two different light conditions. The length of the recorded sequences varied from 700 to 1400 frames per person with an image resolution of 320×240 for thermal and gray images.

7.7.1 Evaluation of Tracking in Thermal Images

To compare the different measurement models we evaluated the tracking performance on the test sequences. In the Particle Filter we used a total of 300 particles, and the weighted mean of the best 20% of all particles of the tracker was compared to the ground truth data for all test sequences. The tracking accuracy TA, detection rate DR, false positive rate FPR and classification rate CR that were described in the last chapter (see section 6.3) were calculated in order to compare the tracking performance of the different methods.

Table 7.2 shows the results of the evaluation. As one can see, the feature based model performs slightly better than the elliptic model. The reason for this is that in some cases the contour model does not fit exactly to the upper body part of the person, which results in a bad estimate for the whole body (see figure 7.11). However, the main disadvantage of using the feature model is that we just get a rough estimate about the position of the upper body part of the person while the contour model gives us the position of the head relative to the body. This information could be necessary for e.g. a face tracking system on a higher level. Therefore, we propose the usage of the combination of both models to achieve the most accurate tracking results. As shown in table 7.2, with the combination of both models we are able to get the highest tracking accuracy with the lowest number of false detections. On an Athlon XP1600 processor, the time for processing one frame with the contour model is 11ms while the feature model requires 7ms for classifier evaluation and 4ms to calculate the integral image. The combination of both models requires 14ms, which is equivalent to a frame-rate of 71 Hz and leaves enough computational resources for other high-level tasks such as planning, navigation, face recognition etc.

Figure 7.11: Comparing three different measurement models in thermal images (left: contour model, middle: feature model, right: combined contour and feature model).

7.7.2   Evaluation of Face Detection and Recognition

The face classifier was trained offline using 4846 images of faces and 7474 non-faces. The final strong classifier consists of 150 features. To test the recognition ability of the system we collected a face database consisting of 8 faces per person that where extracted by the face tracker in the second part of the 17 sequences. The first part had been used as test sequences. We used 500 particles to track the face, and in all sequences the face region was successfully detected and tracked. Due to the fact that Particle Filtering is a stochastic process face tracking and recognition experiments were repeated 5 times on every test sequence. In 41% of all test iterations the face could not be recognized correctly which is mainly due to three problems with using the Eigenface approach:

- Difference in light conditions: some images in the training set had strong light from one side.

- Viewing angle: the algorithm was trained using frontal views of the faces.

- Accuracy of face region cropping: the approach needs a very accurately located and cropped face region.

However, the main focus in this chapter lies on detection and tracking in the thermal image so that the improvement of the recognition step by e.g. using a larger database, which covers more different light conditions, is left for future research. A comparison of different face recognition approaches on mobile robots can be found in [26].

7.8 Summary

In this chapter, one of the first systems to detect and track people in thermal images on a mobile robot was developed. People have a very distinctive profile in thermal images so that robust detection and tracking can be guaranteed even in unconstrained and cluttered environments as well as in complete darkness.

Three different measurement models were compared in this chapter: a contour model that uses two elliptical shapes, which describe the persons head and body part, a gray value feature model that was learned offline on a set of thermal images, and the combination of both models. As thermal images do not provide much texture information, the contour model alone can give good tracking results on the examined test sets. The feature model performs better with the disadvantage of giving only a rough estimate of the person's upper body position. The combination of both models provides the best tracking accuracy, with only slightly increased runtime.

Tracking in thermal images using the proposed measurement models was used to get an estimate about the position of a person in the vicinity of the robot. With the proposed approach, people could be detected up to 7 meters away from the robot and no assumptions had to be made concerning the viewing angle so that people could be tracked in frontal, side and back view as long as they were standing upright. A reactive robot controller used the estimate of the person's position to steer the robot near the person, and a face tracking process was started, which extracts the face region. A standard face recognition approach was implemented in order to identify the person that is next to the robot.

Chapter 8

Conclusions and future work

8.1 Summary

Two fundamental problems in real-time computer vision were studied in this thesis: object detection using offline learned classifiers and object tracking in unconstrained scenarios. Special attention was paid to the problem of developing methods that are able to achieve robust classification and tracking results while running in real-time on standard PC hardware. The algorithms were developed in order to run on embedded systems like mobile robots where the processing time is limited due to hardware constraints and other tasks that are operating at the same time. The task of finding the optimum between robustness on the one hand and runtime performance on the other hand revealed a strong dependency of computer vision and optimization. Therefore, one major focus in this thesis was to incorporate heuristic optimization algorithms like Evolutionary Algorithms and Particle Swarms, which are able to find optima in multi-dimensional and multi-modal search spaces, into the computer vision task.

In the first part of the thesis a new combination of Evolutionary Search and Adaboost was developed and studied on the task of detecting objects in images using offline learned classifiers. It was shown that by the introduction of Evolutionary Search larger sets of features can be searched much faster and yield classifiers with higher robustness. At the same time the online runtime, that was needed for classification, was reduced, which makes the algorithm especially applicable in systems with real-time requirements. A second method that combines Evolutionary Search with Support Vector Classification was proposed and evaluated on the same problem. Here, it was shown that the newly developed crossover and mutation operators that use a feature ranking criterion outperformed the standard algorithm.

The second part of the thesis concentrated on the development of new extensions of the

107

Condensation tracking algorithm. The general conceptual similarities between dynamic search with Evolutionary Algorithms and Condensation were studied and ideas from the field of heuristic optimization (crossover, swarm dynamics) were investigated in more detail. Here, two new ideas were implemented and compared to the standard algorithm: Condensation using a crossover operator and Condensation with swarm dynamics. It was shown that the newly proposed algorithms can improve the tracking performance so that fewer image evaluations were needed for robust tracking. The incorporation of swarm dynamics into the tracking process yielded the best tracking results.

Finally, an application was presented on an autonomous mobile robot in chapter 7, where one of the first mobile systems that is able to detect and track people using a thermal camera was developed. A thermal camera that visualizes heat showed to be a preferred sensor for people tracking since a person can be separated well from the background. A new measurement model was proposed that estimates the position of the head and body of a person with two elliptic shapes. This model was compared with an offline learned feature model, and tracking experiments in an uncontrolled office environment showed that a combination of both models provided the most accurate tracking results while achieving real-time performance on a mobile robot. With the proposed approach it was possible to detect and track a person in frontal, side and back view up to 7 meters away from the robot. The system was completed by a face tracking algorithm in grayscale images, which extracts facial regions, which were used to automatically update the face recognition process over time in order to identify the person that faces the robot.

8.2   Perspectives for future work

The field of optimization techniques in computer vision has much potential for future developments. Some of them that are closely related to the work in this thesis will be pointed out in the following.
The work in chapter 4 concentrated on improving the algorithm that learns a single strong classifier. The proposed methods, however, can be combined with algorithms that learn a detector cascade. The combination as well as the usage of Evolutionary Algorithms for cascade learning could be studied further as well as the application of reduced set SVMs and nonlinear SVMs. All methods are based on features in gray value images, which provide rich information for object detection. However, one can think of unsupervised learning classifiers based on e.g. object shapes. The measurement model that was used in this thesis for tracking people in thermal images was tuned by hand, but it should also be possible to learn contour models from a given training set.

Within the time-frame of this thesis several extensions of the Condensation algorithm using techniques from the field of heuristic optimization have been studied. Evolutionary

Algorithms are also permanently enhanced so that several other ideas (e.g. scout populations [21]) could be studied on tracking problems in the future. It is also imaginable to switch online between different strategies depending on the state of the tracker, the tracking uncertainty and the runtime requirements.

The topic of recognizing objects was only addressed using a standard technique for face recognition in the last chapter. Here, it could be interesting to additionally use thermal images of faces in the database in order to improve the recognition task and to compare different face recognition techniques.

Appendix A

Parameter evaluation of Condensation with Crossover

The results for the evaluation of the parameters of Condensation with Crossover are shown in table A.1 and A.2 in this chapter. A detailed description of the related experiments is given in chapter 6.

Method	#Samples	CR mean ± std	TA mean ± std
CondensationCrossover $p_c = 0.1$	250	1.00 ± 0.00	0.93 ± 0.00
CondensationCrossover $p_c = 0.2$	250	1.00 ± 0.00	0.93 ± 0.00
CondensationCrossover $p_c = 0.3$	250	1.00 ± 0.00	0.92 ± 0.00
CondensationCrossover $p_c = 0.4$	250	1.00 ± 0.00	0.91 ± 0.00
CondensationCrossover $p_c = 0.5$	250	1.00 ± 0.00	0.90 ± 0.00
CondensationCrossover $p_c = 0.6$	250	0.98 ± 0.01	0.88 ± 0.01
CondensationCrossover $p_c = 0.7$	250	0.93 ± 0.03	0.84 ± 0.01
CondensationCrossover $p_c = 0.8$	250	0.85 ± 0.03	0.79 ± 0.01
CondensationCrossover $p_c = 0.1$	100	0.99 ± 0.00	0.90 ± 0.00
CondensationCrossover $p_c = 0.2$	100	1.00 ± 0.00	0.91 ± 0.00
CondensationCrossover $p_c = 0.3$	100	1.00 ± 0.00	0.90 ± 0.00
CondensationCrossover $p_c = 0.4$	100	0.99 ± 0.00	0.89 ± 0.00
CondensationCrossover $p_c = 0.5$	100	0.98 ± 0.02	0.87 ± 0.01
CondensationCrossover $p_c = 0.6$	100	0.94 ± 0.03	0.85 ± 0.01
CondensationCrossover $p_c = 0.7$	100	0.87 ± 0.03	0.81 ± 0.02
CondensationCrossover $p_c = 0.8$	100	0.72 ± 0.05	0.77 ± 0.02
CondensationCrossover $p_c = 0.1$	50	0.96 ± 0.02	0.86 ± 0.01
CondensationCrossover $p_c = 0.2$	50	0.98 ± 0.01	0.87 ± 0.01
CondensationCrossover $p_c = 0.3$	50	0.98 ± 0.01	0.87 ± 0.01
CondensationCrossover $p_c = 0.4$	50	0.96 ± 0.02	0.85 ± 0.01
CondensationCrossover $p_c = 0.5$	50	0.92 ± 0.03	0.83 ± 0.01
CondensationCrossover $p_c = 0.6$	50	0.88 ± 0.05	0.81 ± 0.02
CondensationCrossover $p_c = 0.7$	50	0.76 ± 0.06	0.77 ± 0.02
CondensationCrossover $p_c = 0.8$	50	0.59 ± 0.08	0.73 ± 0.03
CondensationCrossover $p_c = 0.1$	25	0.83 ± 0.04	0.79 ± 0.01
CondensationCrossover $p_c = 0.2$	25	0.86 ± 0.03	0.79 ± 0.02
CondensationCrossover $p_c = 0.3$	25	0.84 ± 0.05	0.79 ± 0.01
CondensationCrossover $p_c = 0.4$	25	0.82 ± 0.04	0.78 ± 0.02
CondensationCrossover $p_c = 0.5$	25	0.79 ± 0.07	0.78 ± 0.02
CondensationCrossover $p_c = 0.6$	25	0.68 ± 0.07	0.75 ± 0.02
CondensationCrossover $p_c = 0.7$	25	0.54 ± 0.06	0.72 ± 0.02
CondensationCrossover $p_c = 0.8$	25	0.41 ± 0.07	0.70 ± 0.02
CondensationCrossover $p_c = 0.1$	15	0.56 ± 0.05	0.73 ± 0.02
CondensationCrossover $p_c = 0.2$	15	0.63 ± 0.08	0.73 ± 0.01
CondensationCrossover $p_c = 0.3$	15	0.62 ± 0.05	0.73 ± 0.02
CondensationCrossover $p_c = 0.4$	15	0.58 ± 0.06	0.73 ± 0.02
CondensationCrossover $p_c = 0.5$	15	0.52 ± 0.08	0.71 ± 0.03
CondensationCrossover $p_c = 0.6$	15	0.39 ± 0.08	0.70 ± 0.03
CondensationCrossover $p_c = 0.7$	15	0.33 ± 0.10	0.68 ± 0.04
CondensationCrossover $p_c = 0.8$	15	0.24 ± 0.05	0.68 ± 0.04

Table A.1: Tracking performance for Condensation with Crossover with different crossover rates p_c and $\sigma_v = 4.0$.

Method	#Samples	CR mean ± std	TA mean ± std
CondensationCrossover $\sigma_v = 1.0$	250	0.91 ± 0.04	0.85 ± 0.02
CondensationCrossover $\sigma_v = 2.0$	250	1.00 ± 0.00	0.91 ± 0.00
CondensationCrossover $\sigma_v = 3.0$	250	1.00 ± 0.00	0.92 ± 0.00
CondensationCrossover $\sigma_v = 4.0$	250	1.00 ± 0.00	0.93 ± 0.00
CondensationCrossover $\sigma_v = 5.0$	250	1.00 ± 0.00	0.93 ± 0.00
CondensationCrossover $\sigma_v = 6.0$	250	1.00 ± 0.00	0.93 ± 0.00
CondensationCrossover $\sigma_v = 7.0$	250	1.00 ± 0.00	0.92 ± 0.00
CondensationCrossover $\sigma_v = 8.0$	250	1.00 ± 0.00	0.92 ± 0.00
CondensationCrossover $\sigma_v = 1.0$	100	0.79 ± 0.04	0.80 ± 0.02
CondensationCrossover $\sigma_v = 2.0$	100	0.96 ± 0.02	0.88 ± 0.01
CondensationCrossover $\sigma_v = 3.0$	100	0.99 ± 0.01	0.90 ± 0.00
CondensationCrossover $\sigma_v = 4.0$	100	1.00 ± 0.00	0.90 ± 0.00
CondensationCrossover $\sigma_v = 5.0$	100	1.00 ± 0.00	0.90 ± 0.00
CondensationCrossover $\sigma_v = 6.0$	100	1.00 ± 0.00	0.90 ± 0.00
CondensationCrossover $\sigma_v = 7.0$	100	1.00 ± 0.00	0.90 ± 0.00
CondensationCrossover $\sigma_v = 8.0$	100	1.00 ± 0.00	0.90 ± 0.00
CondensationCrossover $\sigma_v = 1.0$	50	0.62 ± 0.08	0.76 ± 0.02
CondensationCrossover $\sigma_v = 2.0$	50	0.92 ± 0.03	0.84 ± 0.02
CondensationCrossover $\sigma_v = 3.0$	50	0.97 ± 0.02	0.86 ± 0.01
CondensationCrossover $\sigma_v = 4.0$	50	0.97 ± 0.02	0.87 ± 0.01
CondensationCrossover $\sigma_v = 5.0$	50	0.98 ± 0.02	0.87 ± 0.01
CondensationCrossover $\sigma_v = 6.0$	50	0.98 ± 0.01	0.87 ± 0.01
CondensationCrossover $\sigma_v = 7.0$	50	0.98 ± 0.01	0.87 ± 0.01
CondensationCrossover $\sigma_v = 8.0$	50	0.98 ± 0.01	0.86 ± 0.01
CondensationCrossover $\sigma_v = 1.0$	25	0.38 ± 0.09	0.69 ± 0.04
CondensationCrossover $\sigma_v = 2.0$	25	0.70 ± 0.08	0.76 ± 0.03
CondensationCrossover $\sigma_v = 3.0$	25	0.83 ± 0.04	0.79 ± 0.01
CondensationCrossover $\sigma_v = 4.0$	25	0.87 ± 0.04	0.80 ± 0.01
CondensationCrossover $\sigma_v = 5.0$	25	0.87 ± 0.04	0.80 ± 0.01
CondensationCrossover $\sigma_v = 6.0$	25	0.90 ± 0.02	0.81 ± 0.01
CondensationCrossover $\sigma_v = 7.0$	25	0.89 ± 0.03	0.80 ± 0.01
CondensationCrossover $\sigma_v = 8.0$	25	0.89 ± 0.02	0.81 ± 0.01
CondensationCrossover $\sigma_v = 1.0$	15	0.22 ± 0.07	0.68 ± 0.04
CondensationCrossover $\sigma_v = 2.0$	15	0.42 ± 0.08	0.70 ± 0.03
CondensationCrossover $\sigma_v = 3.0$	15	0.53 ± 0.05	0.71 ± 0.02
CondensationCrossover $\sigma_v = 4.0$	15	0.59 ± 0.06	0.73 ± 0.02
CondensationCrossover $\sigma_v = 5.0$	15	0.63 ± 0.08	0.74 ± 0.02
CondensationCrossover $\sigma_v = 6.0$	15	0.65 ± 0.04	0.74 ± 0.01
CondensationCrossover $\sigma_v = 7.0$	15	0.65 ± 0.04	0.74 ± 0.02
CondensationCrossover $\sigma_v = 8.0$	15	0.66 ± 0.05	0.75 ± 0.02

Table A.2: Tracking performance for Condensation with Crossover with different values for σ_v and $p_c = 0.25$

Bibliography

[1] ActivMediaRobotics Inc., New Hampshire, USA,
URL http://www.mobilerobots.com.

[2] Aria Adavanced Robotics Interface for Applications.
URL http://www.activerobots.com/SOFTWARE/aria.htm.

[3] Infrared Thermal Imager NEC Thermo Tracer TS 7302, Productguide
URL http://www.necsan-ei.co.jp/osd/thermography/catalog/TS7302.pdf.

[4] SICK AG, Düsseldorf, Germany,
URL http://www.sick.de.

[5] The realtime FAQ.
URL http://www.faqs.org/faqs/realtime-computing/faq/.

[6] S. Agarwal and D. Roth. Learning a Sparse Representation for Object Detection.
In *Proceedings of the European Conference on Computer Vision (ECCV)*, pages
113–127, 2002.

[7] H. Andreasson and T. Duckett. Object Recognition by a Mobile Robot using Omni-
Directional Vision. In *Proceedings of the Eighth Scandinavian Conference on Artificial Intelligence*, 2003.

[8] P. Angeline. Evolutionary Optimization versus Particle Swarm Optimization: Phi-
losophy and Performance Differences. In *Proceedings of the 7th Annual Conference of Evolutionary Programming*, pages 601–611, 1998.

[9] P. Angeline. Using Selection to Improve Particle Swarm Optimization. In *IEEE
International Conference of Evolutionary Computation*, pages 84–89, Anchorage,
Alaska, USA, 1998.

[10] C. Bahlmann, Y. Zhu, V. Ramesh, M. Pellkofer, and T.Koehler. A system for traffic
sign detection, tracking, and recognition using color, shape, and motion information. In *IEEE Intelligent Vehicles Symposium (IV 2005)*, pages 255–260, 2005.

[11] J. Bala, K. DeJong, J. Huang, H. Vafaie, and H. Wechsler. Using learning to facilitate the evolution of features for recognizing visual concepts. *Evolutionary Computation*, 4(3):297–312, 1997.

[12] J. Barreto, P. Menezes, and J. Dias. Human-Robot Interaction based on Haar-like Features and Eigenfaces. In *Proc. of the 2004 IEEE International Conference on Robotic and Automation (ICRA 04)*, pages 1888–1893, New Orleans, LA, 2004.

[13] M.S. Bartlett, G. Littlewort, I. Fasel, and J.R. Movellan. Real time face detection and facial expression recognition: Development and application to human-computer interaction. In *CVPR Workshop on Computer Vision and Pattern Recognition for Human-Computer Interaction*, Vancouver, Canada, 2003.

[14] S. Belongie, J. Malik, and J. Puzicha. Matching shapes. In *Proceedings of the International Conference on Computer Vision (ICCV)*, pages 454–461, 2001.

[15] S. Belongie, J. Malik, and J. Puzicha. Shape matching and object recognition using shape contexts. *IEEE Transactions on Pattern Analysis and Machine Intelligence*, 24(4):509–522, 2002.

[16] M. Bertozzi, A. Broggi, P. Grisleri, T. Graf, and M. Meinecke. Pedestrian Detection in Infrared Images. In *Proc. IEEE Intelligent Vehicles Symposium*, pages 662–667, Columbus, USA, 2003.

[17] A. Blake and M. Isard, editors. *Active Contours*. Springer, London, 1998.

[18] J. Blanco, W. Burgard, R. Sanz, and J.L. Fernandez. Fast face detection for mobile robots by integrating laser range data with vision. In *Proceedings of the 11th International Conference on Advanced Robotics (ICAR)*, 2003.

[19] A. Blum and P. Langley. Selection of relevant features and examples in machine learning. *Artificial Intelligence*, 97:245–271, 1997.

[20] L. Bourdev and J. Brandt. Robust Object Detection via Soft Cascade. In *Proceedings of the IEEE Conference on Computer Vision and Pattern Recognition (CVPR)*, volume 2, pages 236–243, 2005.

[21] J. Branke. *Evolutionary Optimization in Dynamic Environments*. PhD thesis, ETH Zürich, 2000.

[22] L. Brèthes, P.Menezes, F. Lerasle, and J.Hayet. Face Tracking and Hand Gesture Recognition for Human-Robot Interaction. In *Proc. of the 2004 IEEE International Conference on Robotic and Automation (ICRA 04)*, pages 1901–1906, New Orleans, LA, 2004.

[23] A. Bue, D. Comaniciu, V. Ramesh, and C. Regazzoni. Smart cameras with real-time video object generation. In *Proceedings of the IEEE International Conference on Image Processing*, volume 3, pages 429–432, 2002.

[24] C. J. C. Burges. Simplified support vector decision rules. In *International Conference on Machine Learning*, pages 71–77, 1996.

[25] T. Bäck. *Evolutionary Algorithms in Theory and Practice.* Oxford University Press, 1996.

[26] H.-J. Böhme, T. Wilhelm, and H.-M. Gross. Gesichtsanalyse für die intuitive Mensch-Roboter-Interaktion. In *Proceedings Autonome Mobile Systeme (AMS)*, pages 67–73, 2005.

[27] P. Carbonetto. Viola training data [Database].
URL http://www.cs.ubc.ca/~pcarbo/viola-traindata.tar.gz.

[28] S. L. Chang, L. S. Chen, Y. C. Chung, and S. W. Chen. Automatic license plate recognition. *IEEE Transactions on Intelligent Transportation Systems*, 5(1):42–53, 2004.

[29] L. Chen, L. Zhang, L. Zhu, M. Li, and H. Zhang. A Novel Facial Feature Point Localization algorithm using Probabilistic-like output. In *Proceedings of the Asian Conference on Computer Vision (ACCV)*, 2004.

[30] G. Cielniak and T. Duckett. Person Identification by Mobile Robots in Indoor Environments. In *Proc. IEEE Int. Workshop on Robotic Sensing (ROSE 2003)*, Örebro, Sweden, 2003.

[31] G. Cielniak, A. Treptow, and T. Duckett. Quantitative performance evaluation of a people tracking system on a mobile robot. In *Proceedings of the European Conference on Mobile Robotics (ECMR)*, pages 182–187, 2005.

[32] A. J. Colmenarez, B. Frey, and T. S. Huang. Detection and Tracking of Faces and Facial Features. In *Proceedings of the International Conference on Image Processing*, pages 657–661, 1999.

[33] A. J. Colmenarez and T. S. Huang. Face detection with information-based maximum discrimination. In *Proceedings of the International Conference on Computer Vision and Pattern Recognition*, pages 782–787, 1997.

[34] C. Cortes and V. Vapnik. Support vector networks. *Machine Learning*, 20:1–25, 1995.

[35] J. Cui and Z. Sun. Vision-based Hand Motion Capture Using Genetic Algorithm. In *Evolutionary Computation in Image and Analysis and Signal Processing*, volume 3005 of *Lecture Notes in Computer Science*, pages 289–300, 2004.

[36] G. N. DeSouza and A. C. Kak. Vision for Mobile Robot Navigation: A Survey. *IEEE Transactions on Pattern Analysis and Machine Intelligence (PAMI)*, 24(2):237–267, 2002.

[37] J. Deutscher, A. Blake, and I. Reid. Articulated body motion capture by annealed particle filtering. In *IEEE Conference on Computer Vision and Pattern Recognition*, pages 126–133, 2000.

[38] J. Deutscher, A. Davison, and I. Reid. Automatic Partitioning of High Dimensional Search Spaces Associated with Articulated Body Motion Capture. In *IEEE Conference on Computer Vision and Pattern Recognition*, pages 669–676, 2001.

[39] A. Doucet, N. de Freitas, and N. Gordon, editors. *Sequential Monte Carlo Methods in Practice*. Springer, New York, 2001.

[40] H. Drucker. Effect of pruning and early stopping on performance of a boosting ensemble. *Computational Statistics and Data Analysis*, 38(4):393–406, 2002.

[41] H. Drucker and C. Cortes. Boosting decision trees. *Advances in Neural Information Processing Systems*, 8:479–485, 1996.

[42] S. Feyrer and A. Zell. Detection, tracking, and pursuit of humans with an autonomous mobile robot. In *Proc. of the IEEE/RSJ International Conference on Intelligent Robots and Systems (IROS)*, pages 864–869, 1999.

[43] S. Feyrer and A. Zell. Robust Real-Time Pursuit of Persons with a Mobile Robot Using Multisensor Fusion. In *6th International Conference on Intelligent Autonomous Systems (IAS-6)*, pages 710–715, Venice, Italy, 2000.

[44] A. Fod, A. Howard, and M. Mataric. Laser-based people tracking. In *Proceedings of the IEEE International Conference on Robotics and Automation (ICRA)*, pages 3024–3029, 2002.

[45] D. B. Fogel. The Advantages of Evolutionary Computation. In *BCEC: Bio-Computing an Emergent Computation*, pages 1–11, 1997.

[46] L. J. Fogel, A. J. Owens, and M. J. Walsh. *Artificial Intelligence through Simulated Evolution*. John Wiley & Sons, New York, 1966.

[47] D. A. Forsyth and J. Ponce. *Computer Vision: A Modern Approach*, chapter 22. Prentice Hall, 2002.

[48] Y. Freund and R. E. Schapire. Experiments with a new boosting algorithm. In *Proceedings of the Thirteenth International Conference on Machine Learning*, pages 148–156, 1996.

[49] Y. Freund and R. E. Schapire. A Decision-Theoretic Generalization of on-line Learning and an Application to Boosting. *Journal of Computer and System Sciences*, 55(1):119–139, 1997.

[50] Y. Freund and R. E. Schapire. A Short Introduction to Boosting. *Journal of Japanese Society for Artificial Intelligence*, 14(5):771–780, 1999.

[51] T. Gal. *Grundlagen des Operations Research 1*. Springer, Berlin, 1991.

[52] M. R. Garey and D. S. Johnson, editors. *Computers and Intractability: A Guide to the Theory of NP-Completeness*. W. H. Freeman, 1979.

[53] M. N. Gibbs. *Bayesian Gaussian Processes for Regression and Classification*. PhD thesis, University of Cambridge, 1997.

[54] A. Guarda, C. Le Gal, and A. Lux. Evolving visual features and detectors. In *International Symposium on Computer Graphics, Image Processing, and Vision*, pages 246–253, 1998.

[55] I. Guyon, J. Weston, S. Barnhill, and V. Vapnik. Gene Selection for Cancer Classification using Support Vector Machines. *Machine Learning*, 46(1-3):389–422, 2002.

[56] H. Rowley, S. Baluja and T. Kanade. Neural network-based face detection. *IEEE Transactions on Pattern Analysis and Machine Intelligence*, 20(1):23–38, January, 1998.

[57] A. Hampapur, L. M. Brown, J. Connell, M. Lu, H. Merkl, S. Pankanti, A. W. Senior, C.F. Shu, and Y.L. Tian. Smart Video Surveillance - Exploring the Concept of Multiscale Spatiotemporal Tracking. *IEEE Transactions on Signal Processing*, 22(2):38–51, 2005.

[58] N. Hansen and A. Ostermeier. Convergence properties of evolution strategies with the derandomized covariance matrix adaptation: The $(\mu/\mu_i, \lambda)$-CMA-ES. In *Proceedings of the 5th European Congress on Intelligent Techniques and Soft Computing*, pages 650–654, 1997.

[59] N. Hansen and A. Ostermeier. Completely derandomized self-adaption in evolution strategies. *Evolutionary Computation*, 9(2):455–492, 2001.

[60] I. Haritaoglu, D. Harwood, and L.S. Davis. W-4: Real-time surveillance of People and Their Activities. *IEEE Transactions on Pattern Analysis and Machine Intelligence*, 22(8):809–830, 2000.

[61] B. Heisele, T. Poggio, and M. Pontil. Face detection in still gray images. Technical Report AI Memo 1687, Massachusetts Institute of Technology, 2000.

[62] B. Heisele, T. Serre, S. Prentice, and T. Poggio. Hierarchical classification and feature reduction for fast face detection with support vector machines. *Pattern Recognition*, 36:2007–2017, 2003.

[63] T. Higuchi. Monte carlo filter using the genetic algorithm operators. *Journal of Statistical Computation and Simulation*, 59:1–23, 1997.

[64] J. H. Holland. *Adaption in Natural and Artificial Systems*. Ann Arbor, 1975.

[65] D. Howard, S. C. Roberts, and R. Brankin. Evolution of ship detectors for satellite SAR imagery. In *Genetic Programming: Second European Workshop EuroGP'99*, pages 135–148, 1999.

[66] M. Isard and A. Blake. Condensation – conditional density propagation for visual tracking. *International Journal of Computer Vision*, 29(1):5–28, 1998.

[67] M. Isard and A. Blake. Icondensation: Unifying low-level and high-level tracking in a stochastic framework. In *Proceedings of the 5th European Conference Computer Vision*, pages 893–908, 1998.

[68] M. Isard and A. Blake. A mixed-state condensation tracker with automatic model switching. In *Proceedings of the 6th International Conference on Computer Vision*, pages 107–112, 1998.

[69] M. J. Jones and P. Viola. Face Recognition using Boosted Local Features. Technical Report TR2003-25, Mitsubishi Electric Research Laboratories Inc. (MERL), 2003.

[70] R. E. Kalman. A new approach to linear filtering and prediction problems. *Transactions of the ASME–Journal of Basic Engineering*, 82(Series D):35–45, 1960.

[71] J. Kennedy and R. C. Eberhart. Particle Swarm Optimization. In *Proceedings of the 1995 IEEE International Conference on Neural Networks Computation*, pages 1942–1948, Perth, Australia, 1995.

[72] J. Kennedy and R. C. Eberhart. *The Particle Swarm: Social Adaptation in Information-Processing Systems*, pages 379–387. McGraw-Hill, London, 1999.

[73] W. Kienzle, G. H. Bakir, M. O. Franz, and B. Schölkopf. Efficient Approximations for Support Vector Machines in Object Detection. In *Proceedings of DAGM 26th Pattern Recognition Symposium*, pages 54–61, 2004.

[74] S. Kirkpatrick, C. D. Gelatt, and M. P. Vecchi. Optimization by simulated annealing. *Science*, 220:671–680, 1983.

[75] R. Kohavi and G. John. Wrappers for feature subset selection. *Artificial Intelligence*, 97(12):273–324, 1997.

[76] J. R. Koza. *Genetic Programming.* MIT Press, Cambridge, MA, 1992.

[77] K. Krawiec and B. Bhanu. Visual learning by evolutionary feature synthesis. In *Twentieth International Conference on Machine Learning (ICML 2003)*, pages 376–383, 2003.

[78] R. A. Krohling. Gaussian Particle Swarm and Particle Filter for Nonlinear State Estimation. In *Proceedings of the 9th IASTED International Conference on Artificial Intelligence and Soft Computing*, pages 399–404, 2005.

[79] S. Lang, M. Kleinhagenbrock, S. Hohenner, J. Fritsch, G. A. Fink, and G. Sagere. Providing the Basis for Human-Robot-Interaction: A Multi-Modal Attention System for a Mobile Robot. In *Proc. Int. Conf. on Multimodal Interfaces*, pages 28–35, Vancouver, Canada, 2003.

[80] D. D. Le and S. Satoh. An Efficient Feature Selection Method for Object Detection. In *Proceedings of the 3rd International Conference on Advances in Pattern Recognition (ICAPR)*, pages 461–468, 2005.

[81] D. D. Le and S. Satoh. Fusion of Local and Global Features for Efficient Object Detection. In *Applications of Neural Networks and Machine Learning in Image Processing*, pages 106–116, 2005.

[82] D. D. Le and S. Satoh. Multi-Stage Approach to Fast Face Detection. In *Proceedings of the British Machine Vision Conference (BMVC)*, pages 769–778, 2005.

[83] G. Lefaix, E. Marchand, and P. Bouthemy. Motion-based obstacle detection and tracking for car driving assistance. In *International Conference on Pattern Recognition, ICPR*, pages 74–77, Québec, Canada, 2002.

[84] P. Li and H. Wang. Probabilistic Object Tracking based on Machine Learning and Importance Sampling. In *Proceedings of the Iberian Conference on Pattern Recognition and Image Analysis*, volume 1, pages 161–167, 2005.

[85] S.Z. Li, Z.Q. Zhang, Harry Shum, and H.J. Zhang. Floatboost learning for classification. In *15-th Annual Conference on Neural Information Processing Systems (NIPS)*, pages 993–1000, 2003.

[86] R. Lienhart, A. Kuranov, and V. Pisarevsky. Empirical analysis of detection cascades of boosted classifiers for rapid object detection. In *Proceedings of DAGM 25th Pattern Recognition Symposium*, pages 297–304, 2003.

[87] R. Lienhart and J. Maydt. An extended set of haar-like features for rapid object detection. In *Proceedings of the International Conference on Image Processing (ICIP)*, pages 900–903, 2002.

[88] Y. Lin and B. Bhanu. Learning features for object recognition. In *Genetic and Evolutionary Computation (GECCO-03)*, pages 2227–2239, 2003.

[89] G. Littlewort, M. S. Bartlett, I. Fasel, J. Chenu, and J. R. Movellan. Analysis of machine learning methods for real-time recognition of facial expression from video. In *CVPR Workshop on Computer Vision and Pattern Recognition for Face Processing*, 2004.

[90] C. Liu and H.Y. Shum. Kullback-Leibler boosting. In *IEEE Conference of Computer Vision and Pattern Recognition (CVPR)*, pages 587–594, 2003.

[91] J. P. MacCormick and A. Blake. A pobabilistic exclusion principle for tracking multiple objects. In *Proceedings of the International Conference on Computer Vision*, pages 572–578, 1999.

[92] J. P. MacCormick and M. Isard. Partitioned sampling, articulated objects and interface-quality hand tracking. In *Proceedings of the European Conference on Computer Vision*, pages 3–19, 2000.

[93] B. McCane and K. Novins. On training cascade face detectors. In *Image and Vision Computing*, pages 239–244, New Zealand, 2003.

[94] U. Meis, W. Ritter, and H. Neumann. Detection and classification of obstacles in night vision traffic scenes based on infrared image. In *Proc. IEEE Intelligent Transportation Systems*, pages 1140–1144, Shanghai, China, 2003.

[95] P. Menezes, L. Brèthes, F. Lerasle, P. Danès, and J. Dias. Visual tracking of silhouettes for human-robot interaction. In *Proceedings of the 11th International Conference on Advanced Robotics (ICAR)*, volume 2, pages 971–976, 2003.

[96] T.B. Moeslund and E. Granum. A survey of computer vision-based human motion capture. *Computer Vision and Image Understanding*, 81:231–268, 2002.

[97] M. Montemerlo, S. Thun, and W. Whittaker. Conditional particle filters for simultaneous mobile robot localization and people-tracking. In *Proceedings of the 10th International Conference on Advanced Robotics (ICAR)*, pages 695–701, 2002.

[98] V. Nair, P. O. Laprise, and J. J. Clark. An FPGA-Based People Detection System. *EURASIP Journal on Applied Signal Processing*, 2005(7):1047–1061, 2005.

[99] H. Nait-Charif and S. J. McKenna. Tracking poorly modeled motion using particle filters with iterated likelihood weighting. In *The Asian Conference on Computer Vision Systems*, pages 156–161, 2004.

[100] H. Nanda and L. Davis. Probabilistic Template based Pedestrian Detection in Infrared Videos. In *IEEE Intelligent Vehicle Symposium*, pages 15–20, Versailles, France, 2002.

[101] K. Nummiaro, E. Koller-Meier, and L. J. Van Gool. An adaptive color-based particle filter. *Image and Vision Computing*, 21(1):99–110, 2003.

[102] K. Okuma, A. Taleghani, N. De Freitas, J.J. Little, and D.G. Lowe. A boosted particle filter: Multitarget detection and tracking. In *Proceedings of the European Conference on Computer Vision*, volume 1, pages 28–39, 2004.

[103] E. Osuna, R. Freund, and F. Girosi. Training support vector machines: An application to face detection. In *Proceedings of the International Conference on Computer Vision and Pattern Recognition*, pages 130–136, 1997.

[104] C. Papageorgiou, M. Oren, and T. Poggio. A General Framework for Object Detection. In *International Conference on Computer Vision*, pages 555–562, 1998.

[105] M. K. Pitt and N. Shephard. Filtering via simulation: Auxiliary Particle Filters. *Journal of the American Statistical Association*, 94(446):590–599, 1999.

[106] J. Poland and A. Zell. Main vector adaptation: A CMA variant with linear time and space complexity. In *Proceedings of the Genetic and Evolutionary Computation Conference*, pages 1050–1055, 2001.

[107] P. Pérez, C. Hue, J. Vermaak, and M. Gangne. Color-based probabilistic tracking. In *European Conference on Computer Vision (ECCV)*, pages 661–675, 2002.

[108] I. Rechenberg. *Evolutionsstrategie: Optimierung technischer Systeme nach Prinzipien der biologischen Evolution*. PhD thesis, Technische Universität Berlin, 1971.

[109] Object recognition from local scale invariant features. D. g. lowe. In *Proceedings of the International Conference on Computer Vision (ICCV)*, pages 1150–1157, 1999.

[110] S. Romdhani, P. H. S. Torr, B. Schölkopf, and A. Blake. Computationally efficient face detection. In *ICCV*, pages 695–700, 2001.

[111] D. Roth, M. Yang, and N.Ahuja. A snowbased face detector. In *Advances in Neural Information Processing Systems 12 (NIPS 12)*, volume 12, pages 855–861, 2000.

[112] G. Rätsch, S. Mika, B. Schölkopf, and K. R. Müller. Constructing Boosting Algorithms from SVMs: An Application to One-Class Classification. *IEEE Transactions on Pattern Analysis and Machine Intelligence*, 24(9):1184–1199, 2002.

[113] M. Rätsch, S. Romdhani, G. Teschke, and Thomas Vetter. Over-Complete Wavelet Approximation of a Support Vector Machine for Efficient Classification. In *Proceedings of DAGM 27th Pattern Recognition Symposium*, pages 351–360, 2005.

[114] M. Rätsch, S. Romdhani, and T. Vetter. Efficient face detection by a cascaded support vector machine using haar-like features. In *DAGM-Symposium*, pages 62–70, 2004.

[115] R. E. Schapire. The Strength of Weak Learnability. *Machine Learning*, 5(2):197–227, 1990.

[116] R. E. Schapire. The Boosting Approach to Machine Learning: An Overview. In *MSRI Workshop on Nonlinear Estimation and Classification*, 2002.

[117] R. E. Schapire, Y. Freund, P. Bartlett, and W. S. Lee. Boosting the margin: A new explanation for the effectiveness of voting methods. *The Annals of Statistics*, 26(5):1651–1686, 1998.

[118] B. Schiele and J. L. Crowley. Recognition without correspondence using multidimensional receptive field histograms. *International Journal of Computer Vision*, 36(1):31–50, 2000.

[119] C. Schlegel, J. Illmann, H. Jaberg, M. Schuster, and R. Wörz. Vision based person tracking with a mobile robot. In *Proceedings of the Ninth British Machine Vision Conference (BMVC)*, pages 418–427, 1998.

[120] C. Schmid and R. Mohr. Local grayvalue invariants for image retrieval. *IEEE Transactions on Pattern Analysis and Machine Intelligence*, 19(5):530–535, 1997.

[121] H. Schneiderman and T. Kanade. A statistical method for object detection applied to faces and cars. In *Proceedings of the International Conference on Computer Vision and Pattern Recognition*, pages 1746–1759, 2000.

[122] H. Schneiderman and T. Kanade. Object detection using the statistics of parts. *International Journal of Computer Vision*, 56(3):151–177, 2004.

[123] H. Schneidermann. *A Statistical Approach to 3D Object Detection Applied to Faces and Cars*. PhD thesis, Carnegie Mellon University, 2000.

[124] D. Schulz, W. Burgard, D. Fox, and A. B. Cremers. People Tracking with Mobile Robots Using Sample-based Joint Probabilistic Data Association Filters. *International Journal of Robotics Research*, 22(2):99–116, 2003.

[125] H. Schwenk and Y. Bengio. Boosting neural networks. *Neural Computation*, 12(8):1869–1887, 2000.

[126] A. Shashua, Y. Gdalyahu, and G. Hayon. Pedestrian detection for driving assistance systems: Single-frame classification and system level performance. In *Proceedings of the IEEE Intelligent Vehicles Symposium*, pages 1–6, Parma, Italy, 2004.

[127] Y. Shi and R. C. Eberhart. A Modified Particle Swarm Optimizer. In *IEEE International Conference of Evolutionary Computation*, pages 69–73, Anchorage, Alaska, USA, 1998.

[128] P. Silapachote, D. R. Karuppiah, and A. R. Hanson. Feature Selection Using AD-ABOOST for Face Expression Recognition. In *IASTED International Conference on Visualization, Imaging, and Image Processing*, pages 84–89, 2004.

[129] A. R. Smith. Color gamut transform pairs. In *SIGGRAPH*, pages 12–19, 1978.

[130] K. Smith and D. Gattica-Perez. Order matters: A distributed sampling method for multi-object tracking. In *Proceedings of the British Machine Vision Conference*, pages 25–32, 2004.

[131] W. M. Spears. Crossover or mutation? In *Foundations of Genetic Algorithms*, pages 221–237, 1993.

[132] J. Sun, J. M. Rehg, and A. F. Bobick. Automatic Cascade Training with Perturbation Bias. In *IEEE Conference of Computer Vision and Pattern Recognition (CVPR)*, pages 276–283, 2004.

[133] Z. Sun, G. Bebis, and R. Miller. Object detection using feature subset selection. *Pattern Recognition*, 37:2165–2176, 2004.

[134] Z. Sun, G. Bebis, and R. Miller. On-road Vehicle Detection Using Evolutionary Gabor Filter Optimization. *IEEE Transactions on Intelligent Transportation Systems*, 6(2):125–137, 2005.

[135] Z. Sun, G. Bebis, and R. Miller. On-road Vehicle Detection: A review. *IEEE Transactions on Pattern Analysis and Machine Intelligence*, 28(5):694–711, 2006.

[136] K. Sung and T. Poggio. Example-based learning for view-based face detection. *IEEE Transactions on Pattern Analysis and Machine Intelligence*, 20:39–51, 1998.

[137] E. A. H. Tito, M. M. B. R. Vellasco, and M.A.C. Pacheco. Genetic particle filter: An evolutionary perspective of smc methods. Technical report, Department of Electrical Engineering, University of Rio De Janeiro, 2003.

[138] P. Torma and C. Szepesvári. Efficient Object Tracking in Video Sequences by means of LS-N-IPS. In *Proceedings of the Second International Symposium on Image and Signal Processing and Analysis*, pages 277–282, 2001.

[139] P. Torma and C. Szepesvári. LS-N-IPS: An Improvement of Particle Filters by means of Local Search. In *Non-linear Control Systems*, 2001.

[140] A. Treptow, G. Cielniak, and T. Duckett. Active people recognition using thermal and grey images on a mobile security robot. In *Proceedings of the IEEE International Conference on Intelligent Robots and Systems (IROS)*, pages 2103–2108, 2005.

[141] A. Treptow, G. Cielniak, and T. Duckett. Comparing measurement models for tracking people in thermal images on a mobile robot. In *Proceedings of the European Conference on Mobile Robotics (ECMR)*, pages 146–151, 2005.

[142] A. Treptow, G. Cielniak, and T. Duckett. Real-Time People Tracking for Mobile Robots using Thermal Vision. *Robotics and Autonomous Systems*, pages 729–739, 2006.

[143] A. Treptow, B. Huhle, and A. Zell. Robot guidance navigation with stereo-vision and a limited field of view. In *Proceedings of the 19th Autonomous Mobile Systems (AMS)*, pages 279–285, 2005.

[144] A. Treptow, A. Masselli, and A. Zell. Real-time object tracking for soccer-robots without color information. In *Proceedings of the European Conference on Mobile Robotics (ECMR)*, pages 33–38, 2003.

[145] A. Treptow and A. Zell. Combining adaboost learning and evolutionary search to select features for real-time object detection. In *Proceedings of the IEEE Congress on Evolutionary Computation (CEC)*, volume 2, pages 2107–2113, 2004.

[146] A. Treptow and A. Zell. Object Tracking for Soccer-Robots without Color Information. *Robotics and Autonomous Systems*, 48(1):41–48, 2004.

[147] M. Turk and A. Pentland. Eigenfaces for Recognition. *Journal of Cognitive Neuroscience*, 3(1):71–86, 1991.

[148] D. Tweed and A. Calway. Tracking many objects using subordinated condensation. In *Proceedings of the British Machine Vision Conference*, pages 283–292, 2002.

[149] L. G. Valiant. A Theory of the Learnable. *Communications of the ACM*, 27(11):1134–1142, 1984.

[150] V. Vapnik, editor. *The Nature of Statistical Learning Theory*. Springer, New York, 1995.

[151] V. Vapnik, editor. *Statistical Learning Theory*. John Wiley and Sons, Inc., New York, 1998.

[152] J. Vermaak, A. Doucet, and P. Pérez. Maintaining multi-modality through mixture-tracking. In *Proceedings of the International Conference on Computer Vision*, pages 1110–1116, 2003.

[153] P. Viola, M. J. Jones, and D. Snow. Detecting Pedestrians Using Patterns of Motion and Appearance. In *Proceedings of the International Conference on Computer Vision (ICCV)*, pages 734–741, 2003.

[154] P. A. Viola and M. J. Jones. Fast and Robust Classification using Asymmetric AdaBoost and a Detector Cascade. In *Neural Information Processing Systems (NIPS)*, pages 1311–1318, 2001.

[155] P. A. Viola and M. J. Jones. Rapid Object Detection using a Boosted Cascade of Simple Features. In *Proceedings of the IEEE Conference on Computer Vision and Pattern Recognition (CVPR)*, volume 1, pages 511–518, 2001.

[156] P. A. Viola and M. J. Jones. Robust Real-Time Object Detection. In *Proceedings of the IEEE Workshop on Statistical and Computational Theories of Computer Vision*, 2001.

[157] P. A. Viola and M. J. Jones. Robust Real-Time Face Detection. *International Journal of Computer Vision*, 57(2):137–154, 2004.

[158] G. Welch and G. Bishop. An Introduction to the Kalman Filter. Technical Report TR 95-041, University of North Carolina, Dept. of Computer Science, 1995.

[159] T. Wilhelm, H.-J. Böhme, and H.-M. Gross. A Multi-Modal System for Tracking and Analyzing Faces on a Mobile Robot. *Robotics and Autonomous Systems*, 48(1):31–40, 2004.

[160] C. Wong, D. Kortenkamp, and M. Speich. A Mobile Robot that Recognizes People. In *Proceedings of the Seventh International Conference on Tools with Artificial Intelligence*, pages 346–353, 1995.

[161] J. Wu, J. M. Rehg, and M. D. Mullin. Learning a Rare Event Detection Cascade by Direct Feature Selection. In *Neural Information Processing Systems (NIPS)*, 2004.

[162] Y. Wu. Vision-Based Gesture Recognition: A Review. In *Proceedings of the International Gesture Workshop*, pages 103–115, 2000.

[163] Y. Wu and T. S. Huang. A Co-inference Approach to Robust Visual Tracking. In *Proceedings of the IEEE International Conference on Computer Vision*, pages 26–33, 2001.

[164] R. Xiao, M.J. Li, and H.J. Zhang. Robust Multi-Pose Face Detection in Images. *IEEE Transactions on Circuits and Systems for Video Technology*, 14(1):31–41, 2004.

[165] R. Xiao, L. Zhu, and H.J. Zhang. Boosting Chain Learning for Object Detection. In *IEEE International Conference on Computer Vision (ICCV)*, pages 709–715, 2003.

[166] F. Xu, X. Liu, and K. Fujimura. Pedestrian Detection and Tracking with Night Vision. *IEEE Transactions on Intelligent Transportation System*, 5(4), 2004.

[167] M. H. Yang, D. J. Kriegman, and N. Ahuja. Detecting faces in images: A survey. *Pattern Analysis and Machine Intelligence (PAMI)*, 24(1):34–58, 2002.

[168] P. Yang, S. Shan, W. Gao, S. Z. Li, and D. Zhang. Face Recognition Using Ada-Boosted Gabor Features. In *IEEE International Conference on Automatic Face and Gesture Recognition*, pages 356–361, 2004.

[169] W. Zajdel, Z. Zivkovic, and B. Krose. Keeping track of humans: Have I seen this person before? In *Proceedings of the IEEE International Conference on Robotics and Automation (ICRA)*, pages 2093–2098, 2005.

[170] L. Zhang, S. Z. Li, Z. Y. Qua, and X. Huang. Boosting Local Feature Based Classifiers for Face Recognition. In *Conference on Computer Vision and Pattern Recognition Workshop*, volume 5, pages 87–92, 2004.

[171] W. Zhang and G. Zelinsky. Current Advances in Computer-based Object Detection and Target Acquisition. Technical Report EYECOG-04-01, State University of New York, 2004.

[172] W. Zhao, R. Chellappa, R. J. Philips, and A. Rosenfeld. Face Recognition: A Literature Survey. *ACM Computing Surveys (CSUR)*, 35(4):399–458, 2003.